GATZ,

IN T

WORDS I HOPE YOU
DISCOVER/EXPERIENCE:
- JOY
- LAUGHTER
- CHALLENGE
- PEACE
- LOVE,
    AND/OR
        INSPIRATION!
    ENJOY,
    Shelly McNAMARA

Praise for *No Blanks, No Pauses*

"Weaving her life story with beautiful poetry, Shelly McNamara encourages all of us to think deeply about the direction of our lives and the relationships that count. Shelly's introspection, gratitude, and most of all, courage, should remind everyone what really matters, today and every day."

> – Katie Couric, Founder, Katie Couric Media

"In *No Blanks, No Pauses*, Shelly McNamara exemplifies the personal growth and resilience that comes with living a mindful life, an authentic life. Acceptance and understanding are essential to growing tolerant, compassionate, empathic, and ultimately loving organizations and communities. Through her personal stories, Shelly shares a compelling, heart-led path forward for each of us to follow to become our best selves. It is essential reading for all leaders who strive to create thriving, productive teams."

> – Arianna Huffington, Founder and CEO, Thrive Global

"I have never read anything that comes close to interweaving such frank and compelling stories of the challenge of growing up . . . of simply growing . . . with deeply insightful and inspiring poems that imbue these stories and their lessons with even greater meaning. What's more, these poems, exceptionally concise and evocative, will live on in memory."

> – John Pepper, former CEO and Chairman, Procter & Gamble

"By sharing the significant events that have shaped her life in *No Blanks, No Pauses*, Shelly McNamara shows us how to accept, understand, and be transformed by love and loss. McNamara's belief in the goodness of human beings and her desire to make all that she encounters better than it was is inspiring. Her story will serve as a model to any of us—no matter what our age, gender, sexuality, social class, race/ethnicity, or nationality—who must look hardship in the eye and view it as an occasion for personal growth and a truer self."

– Dr. Mahzarin R. Banaji, Richard Clarke Cabot Professor of Social Ethics, Harvard University

"The idea of acceptance, love, and understanding of a family to members of the LGBTQ+ community is often either a dream we never achieve or something we have to create ourselves through a family of choice. In her book, Shelly shares her loving yet painfully honest story of how having a loving (and large!) family can pave the way to creating one's own beautiful family—and importantly, how such connection and empathy can translate into leadership in the business community and the world."

– Todd Sears, Founder and CEO, Out Leadership

"Shelly's personal stories illustrate and teach that with the passing of a loved one, there is also an opportunity for a rebirth to occur from within. A rebirth that gives us a chance to step into our purpose to drive impact in the world while honoring the life of those we loved and lost. Thank you, Shelly, for sharing your personal stories with the world, and thank you for giving me a personal invitation to heal."

– Teneshia Jackson-Warner, CEO, Egami Group

"*No Blanks, No Pauses* is a powerful appeal for self-reflection and collective transformation. Through poignant stories and poems, Shelly McNamara shares compelling and timely insights, enjoining each of us to recognize our personal role in bringing about a more compassionate, loving, and equitable world."

– Alyse Nelson, Cofounder, President, and CEO, Vital Voices Global Partnership

"Whether you are a business leader, colleague, friend, or family member—in other words, a human being—this book is for you. Shelly's rise from the youngest in a family of fifteen to Chief Equality & Inclusion Officer at P&G is nothing short of remarkable. Her drive, courage, and compassion for all has fueled both her personal and professional growth. Deeply authentic and personal, this is a book about love. Shelly is a voice for anyone who has ever been made to feel 'less than.' Her wisdom and courage are inspirations for all of us to be better human beings."

— Ed Shirley, Chairman, Sysco

"Shelly McNamara's book *No Blanks, No Pauses* is a story about resilience, determination, love, and support that proves we are all so much alike, even when we're different. Not many of us are the youngest of fifteen children, brought up by a single mother, and yet make it to become the Chief Equality & Inclusion Officer at P&G. She is a role model for every man, woman, and child as she is as true to herself as she is to others. Yet, her story is an approachable one. She is so transparent in her recollections that, as a reader, you feel like you know her even though you've never met her. Shelly McNamara's story is one that must be told, read, and shared broadly. It can save a life, inspire love and forgiveness, and teach us all that a family is a family, no matter what it looks like . . . and love wins—always."

— Lisette Arsuaga, Cofounder, Alliance for Inclusive and Multicultural Marketing (AIMM)

"I'm grateful to see Shelly release a book that reflects on a life lived with intention, reflection, and most of all, loving leadership. Shelly is not only an advocate for LGBTQ youth, but an advocate for compassion and equality—two values that we hold dear at The Trevor Project."

— Amit Paley, CEO and Executive Director, The Trevor Project

"Through masterful storytelling and soul-stirring poetry, Shelly invites us into her journey of self-love and love of others. Along the way, she shows us the immense power of acceptance, compassion, care, and forgiveness. Then, ever so gently, she nudges us to examine our own journeys and encourages us to look for additional ways that we might love and live better lives."

– Janet Reid, PhD, Author of *Intrinsic Inclusion: Rebooting Your Biased Brain*

"Creating a diverse, equal, and just society can only be accomplished through bold, courageous, and passionate people. Through *No Blanks, No Pauses*, we experience the very personal, very real journey of one of these leaders who is driving positive change both within and outside the walls of one of the biggest companies in the world. Incredibly timely, Shelly McNamara's life stories shed light on the experience of marginalization, discrimination, fear, and despair—providing important and deeply personal perspective on an experience known by too many. Shelly's storytelling illuminates the pain in the struggle as well as the freedom and peace that come when you live a life of authenticity and purpose that is committed to lifting up others."

– Patrice Louvet, President and CEO, Ralph Lauren Corporation

No Blanks,
No Pauses

A Path to Loving
Self and Others

Shelly McNamara

www.amplifypublishing.com

No Blanks, No Pauses: A Path to Loving Self and Others

©2021 Shelly McNamara. All Rights Reserved. No part of this publication may be reproduced, stored in a retrieval system or transmitted in any form by any means electronic, mechanical, or photocopying, recording or otherwise without the permission of the author.

I have tried to recreate events, locales, and conversations from my memories of them. In order to maintain their anonymity in some instances I have changed the names of individuals and places. I may have changed some identifying characteristics and details such as physical properties, occupations, and places of residence.

For more information, please contact:
Amplify Publishing
620 Herndon Parkway, Suite 320
Herndon, VA 20170
info@amplifypublishing.com

Library of Congress Control Number: 2020915973

CPSIA Code: PRFRE1120A
ISBN-13: 978-1-64307-486-3

Printed in Canada

I dedicate this book to all who make it part of their life's work to expand respect, equality, and love.

Table of Contents

Foreword: Finding Your Path   1
Marc Pritchard, Chief Brand Officer, Procter & Gamble

1. Who I Am   5

2. Compelled to Write, Driven to Speak   23

3. Regret & Redemption   35

4. Love More. Judge Less.   51

5. The Day Will Come   63

6. Level Set   71

7. The Power of Choice   93

8. Privileges Granted—or Not   105

9. Connected by Love   117

10. Reflections   127

Acknowledgments   137

Original Poems   143

Foreword: Finding Your Path

On March 7, 2012, the path of my life journey changed, although I didn't know it at the time. I had the privilege of introducing a gifted storyteller and a remarkable human being as a speaker at an event in Procter & Gamble's headquarters. The auditorium was packed with employees, and the event was streamed to many locations around the world. This speech represented one of the most powerful and moving moments anyone in the audience had ever experienced. It changed the course of acceptance, inclusion, and equality at our company. It changed many lives, including mine, forever.

The speaker was Shelly McNamara: author of this book, master storyteller and poet; daughter to a mother as close to a saint as a person can be; sister to fourteen siblings; aunt to dozens of nieces and nephews; wife to Cindy, the love of her life; mother to Ali, Kate, and Nicole; "out" business leader at a giant corporation; mentor to hundreds; and dear friend to countless souls, of which I'm honored to be one.

The event was momentous because Shelly told her story publicly for the first time.

One might think that the significant part was "coming out" in front of thousands of people. That was an exceptionally courageous action. But equally powerful were the important lessons of humanity and inspiration expressed in every story Shelly shared—stories and lessons that are now explored in greater depth and with extraordinary insight in every chapter of this book.

There are stories of feeling "less than" because of who you are—whether gay or any other identity or circumstance subject to hurtful bias—and the lesson of "level setting" to see each of us as different yet equally magnificent.

There are stories about the loss of loved ones—an inevitable part of life—and the lesson of finding meaning in each relationship during those moments of pain to help find purpose for why you are here on this Earth.

There are stories of regret—most poignantly told about an absent father who unsuccessfully dealt with his pain through alcohol—and the lesson of forgiveness that sets you free from the shackles of resentment.

There are stories of judgment—difficult enough when experienced personally, but even more searing when experienced through the pain of your children—and the lesson of love as the uniting force that connects all humanity and overcomes exclusion. "Love more, judge less."

There are stories about choice—of living life with authenticity over shame, despite consequences—and the lesson of making choices from a place of love to live true to who you are. "No blanks, no pauses"—only love and recognition of who you are—finding the path of loving self and others.

Through these masterfully told stories enriched with beautiful poems and reflections for consideration, Shelly shines a light on the journey of finding her purpose in life—to open hearts, open minds, and build connections that heal the world. The chapters in the book can serve as a guide for life's journey for anyone at any stage. Shelly's words are a light that shines on all, each word written with love, inspiring the reader with insight and generosity.

Which brings me back to the path of my life journey. Although I introduced Shelly at the 2012 event, I had met her several years before, in 2005. She had told me the story of who she is and about Cindy, her children, and how she chose to live her life authentically and with purpose. We are now colleagues in corporate leadership roles, partnering to achieve equality and inclusion in our company, industry, and society.

It was during the moments in the event when Shelly spoke so beautifully that I realized she had come into my life for a reason—to help me find my path to meaning, mission, and purpose. It started to become clear that the privileges bestowed upon me, deserving or not, are to be used for good. I have since made a life choice to be useful as a force for good, to promote equality, inclusion, and love for all humanity—regardless of gender, sexual orientation or gender identity, race or ethnicity, ability, socioeconomic status, spirituality, or age. This book helped me discover deeper insight about my own journey, strengthening my passion and commitment to that mission. I encourage you, reader, to use it to discover something that supports you in finding your path.

Marc Pritchard
Chief Brand Officer, Procter & Gamble
May 2020

Deep Insight

Deep insight is rarely
Born out of privilege
It comes from
Experiencing the pain
Caused by others—or
The misgivings of life

Listen closely
Listen intently
To the voices
Of those who cry out

They sit along the edges
Outside the circle
Of privilege

Deep insight they bring
How we can all
Be more human
More loving—more giving

Deep insight is rarely
Born out of privilege

1. Who I Am

Deep insight is rarely born out of privilege.

I am a daughter, sister, aunt, mother, wife, storyteller, and "out" business leader at one of the largest Fortune 500 companies in the world. I have learned and experienced much, but *love* stands out above all else.

I am the *daughter* of Helen Louise McNamara. She was a single parent for many years, as my father, Bernard Joseph McNamara was mostly absent. It was his absence, not his presence, that was instrumental in shaping my family and the trajectory of our lives. My mother and father had fifteen children in twenty years, during which my mother was a labor and delivery nurse—convenient, right?! My father left my mother to raise fourteen children on her own and pick up the shattered pieces he left behind.

My mother raised us on the west side of Cleveland, in the community of Lakewood, Ohio. She loved me—and all of her children—without condition, without labels. She simply loved. She truly was the glue that held together our crazy, large family, guiding nine girls and six boys through the chaos that came with living under one roof. Her journey, and the story of my family, laid the foundation for my life.

In 1964, 1516 Grace Avenue became our home only months after I was born, the fifteenth child. The change was well-received; my sister, Mary Ellen, had passed away in our previous home, which left an aura of pain Mom likely wanted to escape.

Grace Avenue, an appropriate name: Mom needed God's grace to raise fourteen children into responsible, loving adulthood. Our home was a lot like a busy train station; there were people moving in many different directions all at once. Some were moving at a fast pace and with purpose, going to school, work, or out to a social event. Others sat around lounging, resting, or engaging in conversations. Our house maintained a pace and frenzy unmatched by any home I have ever visited, chaotic at times and semi-orderly at others. I likely saw and heard things well beyond my years, but it all prompted me to mature quickly and build my own path. Train stations may be loud and chaotic, but they provide a wide range of options for launching your personal journey.

The front lawn doubled as a sports field (mostly for soccer and football), though "lawn" is a bit overstated—it was a nearly barren plot of dirt with just a little grass. It was in my front yard that I learned to hit a tennis ball, catch a football, and be a member of a team. My brother Tom, two years my senior, included me in every game and every sport, gender not relevant. Our games frequently spilled into the street and farther. One of my strongest memories from childhood is the day we held a mini-march and rally in front of our neighbors' home directly across the street, protesting with signs and chants. They'd taken our football after it had landed on their lawn a few times more than they'd liked. Our incessant retrieval of the football was ruining their lawn, or so they said.

Our neighbors in the house next to us had a basketball court that they generously allowed us to use any time. That basketball court was a lifeline for me. I played countless games with Tom and his friends. They pushed me, blocked my shots, and mocked me, just as they did all of the kids (mostly boys) on the court. I built a foundation of strength, confidence, and resilience by being in the game with those boys. Here, I learned to fall and get back up, to lose and play again the next day, and to practice my shots, day after day, until I made them. Tom coached me, encouraged me, and relentlessly supported me. Back then, I thought he was preparing me to be a basketball player; in fact, he was preparing me for life.

As you opened the door into the entryway of 1516 Grace Avenue, directly in front of you was a bench seat that opened to serve as a storage bin for our (singular) baseball bat, football, baseball, and a few baseball gloves. It was also a great place to sit and change my shoes or wait for a friend to arrive. From that seat, I could look directly out of our glass-windowed door to watch the games being played on our front lawn or in the street. The front yard, the bench seat, and those few articles of sports equipment served as anchors for my early years.

The first floor also included a living room and dining room, which were mostly clad in (quite unattractive) army green colored carpeting (mostly because there was a hole worn right down the center). That carpeting took quite a beating, with so many kids coming in and out of our home, regularly holding wrestling matches and football games in the center of our home. The gaping hole was normal to me; I didn't give it much thought back then, as we had many other challenges to keep our attention.

At the back of the first floor was our "TV room," a small room with a small television. We piled many kids into that room to watch shows and movies. In those days, we didn't have a remote; we started off changing the channel with a dial on the television, but when that dial broke from overuse, we changed channels with a set of pliers that sat on the table next to the television set. As the youngest two children, Tom and I usually watched weekend shows like *Fantasy*

Island and *The Love Boat* just the two of us. We loved those rare weekend nights when Mom wasn't working and could relax with us in the TV room. Wednesdays offered me the rare opportunity to watch *The After School Movie* on ABC all by myself in our TV room. These movies, stories about human challenges and redemption with messages about love, life, and humanity, were perfect viewing for this deeply sensitive child who would one day rely on those very insights.

The kitchen sat in the back right corner of the house: modest counter space, a few cupboards, a dishwasher that never worked (but served as a nice hiding spot for snacks), and a table that fit three or four people comfortably. From the kitchen table, I could see our backyard: a gravel driveway, a garage that was too unsafe and unstable to store our one car, and grass that was always overgrown.

For holiday dinners, we had a "little kids table" and a "big kids table." As the fifteenth child, I seemingly never escaped my status as one of the young ones; I don't remember ever making it to the big kids table. On any given weeknight, though, you would find four to six of us kids tightly squeezed around the kitchen table, eating dinner together. We always ate dinner together. The "we" varied based on who was home, but dinner was our one substantive meal of the day and not to be missed if you were home. Tom and I were always at dinner; our siblings Fran, Patrick, Tim, Loretta, Jean, and Nancy were our most frequent dinner partners, but they were not all consistently present. They would often choose one of the two other options: to eat at work or with a friend's family. Their absence from our dinner table helped to ensure the rest of us had enough food to eat. I can see that now.

The second floor, what we called "the upstairs," had five bedrooms. I shared a room with three of my sisters, Nancy, Jean, and Loretta. Our room had two double beds with mattresses that sagged in the middle and blankets that never seemed warm enough. Nancy took up more of the bed than I wanted, and my sisters often came home late at night, making noise that woke me out of a deep sleep. But we had beds and a room to sleep in; we valued that and never took those things, or each other, for granted. We learned to share, compromise, and laugh a lot. We learned to be grateful for the little things. I felt loved.

We also had an attic (or third floor, as we called it). It was quite small, with a low, slanted ceiling, but large enough to hold two single mattresses on the floor. My mother had an enormously gracious and generous heart; I recall a few family friends and relatives needing a temporary home who Mom invited to live in our attic for weeks or months at a time. There was always a range of human beings in and out of our home, as my mother welcomed and loved anyone in need.

I have deep gratitude for my life at 1516 Grace Avenue. I grew immensely from the chaos, and the wide spectrum of humanity that lived in and visited my childhood home. I had love and support that came in many forms. My best friend in the neighborhood was most likely Mrs. Lou Keim, my childhood friend Mary Jo's mother. We often sat and talked on the Keim family porch for hours on end. This ritual began when I was five years old, and lasted well into my teenage years. She served as a life mentor and second mother to me in my younger years. She liked to tell me that I was an old soul in a little body. It is in hindsight that I see her as my best neighborhood friend.

My mother, a nurse, worked the night shift from 3:00 to 11:30 pm because it paid the highest wage. She disliked being away from us five out of seven nights a week. I disliked it, too. As a young child, I frequently asked my mother why she had to go to work again. Mom's reply? "Shelly, I have to put food on the table." It was really that simple to her.

Mom didn't have the time or energy to keep track of each of her fourteen children at every moment. She would designate one of the older kids to be the babysitter, the stand-in person-in-charge. This was a difficult and undesirable job typically held by one of my sisters. Who would want to deal with a houseful of teenagers and their friends? What teenager wants to be disciplined by their older sibling? During my high school years, that unlucky person-in-charge was my sister Loretta. She had the unfortunate task of keeping Tom and his friends in line. They would often gather at our house to play cards and drink beer (the drinking age was eighteen for low-grade beer). The noise level escalated as the empty beer cans mounted. I never envied her position, and knew there was great privilege in being the youngest child: I didn't have younger siblings to care for.

We kept an "out list" by the front door. We were each responsible for adding our name to the list when we left for the evening and crossing it out upon return. On weekends, when she came home at midnight, Mom would ask me to check each bedroom and take inventory of who was in and out of the house. Managing that list became one of several family tasks that I was eager to take off of Mom's shoulders. I loved to make her proud by doing something, anything, to lighten her load.

My mother's schedule was fairly consistent: she had every other weekend off from work, which included Saturday and Sunday. (On the other two weekends, she was off from work on Friday.) I loved her free weekends. We didn't do anything particularly special, but on those two days, *everything* was special because I had time with my mother. I recall helping her with the laundry and attending 4:30 pm Mass on Saturday with her so that we could sleep in on Sunday morning. The simple things became my favorite things—weekends, Sunday dinner, church, and grocery shopping on "Payday Friday."

Feeding fourteen children was quite a task; Payday Friday, twice a month, was a reprieve of sorts. The financial strain and disappointment of "doing without" was a little less visible on Payday Friday weekends. Our trips to the grocery store were so much better. Our refrigerator and cupboards were just a bit more filled with food. Our glasses were more likely to be filled with real milk, not powdered milk. Two days a month, we could buy "pop" (usually three or four two-liter bottles of Pepsi or 7-Up), a bag of pretzels, and maybe a bag of chocolate chip cookies. Given how fast snacks went in my house, my brother Tom and I often took it upon ourselves to "hide" a few of the snacks so that we could have them on another day. Sneaky but true! I loved these special treats, but I particularly recall the joy and relief that I saw on Mom's face on those days. Sunday dinners following Payday Fridays were more complete—roast beef, mashed potatoes, and fresh (not canned) vegetables. Never a drop of food left after those meals. Mom always seemed calm and peaceful on these days.

Mom was proud. Mom was loving. She was a model of endless love, loyalty, and laughter. She was devoted to her family, God, and her patients. She was always taking care of somebody or something. Her days were filled with household chores—grocery shopping, laundry, and cooking. Given that five days a week she left for work at 2:30 pm and returned at midnight, we often came home from school to notes on the kitchen table that read something like this:

Chicken in the fridge
Heat at 375 degrees for 45 minutes
Canned corn on the counter
Mom

On her to-do list, you would also find "Pick up the good nuns on my way to work." Sister Eileen, Sister Margaret, Sister Kathleen: Mom worked at a Catholic hospital and made it her responsibility to drive one or two nuns to work each day. When I asked her why she added this to her already hectic schedule, she would say, "I am hoping that the good nuns will put in a good word for me with the Big Guy in heaven, Shelly. I might need that."

My parents were legally separated for more than fifteen years, but never divorced. Divorce was unacceptable in the Catholic church and not an option Mom would consider. Though her husband was a toxic alcoholic, she feared that God might not forgive her for asking him to leave. Driving the nuns was a bit of "proactive penance" in case God viewed her choice to separate as unacceptable. A loving, devoted mother and nurse—it saddens me to know how deeply she feared judgment.

A core part of my mother's identity was being Catholic. She referred to herself as a devout Catholic. Her faith was immensely important to her, but overall, at the core, she was about love. The dogma was simply her way of articulating it, as was common so many years ago. That was the only way she knew to connect to God . . . through a specific religion and set of rules. My mom believed there was one, narrow pathway to God, owned by and available to a few. Her church taught her that; the culture around her taught her that. She was born in 1919; she was a reflection of her time and generation. I have come to believe that we all have the gateway to God, and there are many pathways to those "pearly gates."

Attending church regularly was important to Mom. It was also important to me, and it was something we typically did just the two of us. We didn't sing well or put much money in the collection basket, but we showed up regularly. Mom instilled in me a deep faith in and love for God that has never wavered, though my personal beliefs have evolved. I believed then, as I do now, that a higher power guides us in the spirit of love and wants for us to celebrate our births, lives beyond this earth, and the communities of which we are a part. I don't believe that a particular dogma or religion has the gateway to God; I believe it is available to all of us. I believe that faith, religion, and spirituality are personal, and need space for personal choice. I have not and I will not tell another how to believe nor what to believe in any arena, particularly one as personal as faith.

Mom carried the responsibility of raising fourteen children on a nurse's wage with a joyful, loving heart. The burden was visible, though, after a full day of mothering and an eight-hour nursing shift. I adored my mother and was keenly aware of how great this burden was. I rarely saw it on her face, but do recall one day and one conversation that has stayed with me for life. I overheard her speaking with a family member who had made a bad financial decision which Mom believed she would need to cover. She said something like, "I don't have the money to cover that. I don't know what I will do. I am afraid that the bank will come after me and my wages."

I looked around the corner to see tears rolling down her soft, worn cheeks. All of nine or ten, I ran into the other room, deciding that this was more than I could understand or handle. Yet I also wanted so desperately to save my mother from this pain that I stuffed down my own fear that we might lose our home and deepened my resolve to *never* be a problem for my mother. I would take care of myself. Mom reinforced this desire in me each time she told me, "Shelly, you are smart. You can be anything you want to be. Don't get financially stuck like I did. You can do better."

We *all* tried to protect Mom. We protected her from anything and everything that might add strain or stress. There was one very important rule that my siblings repeated quite often: "Don't ask Mom for anything!"

I began babysitting at the age of eleven, which provided me some spending money; however, there were times that I just needed or wanted something my meagre budget couldn't cover. During my early teenage years, my friends had a ritual of going to McDonald's for lunch every Friday. If my babysitting money dried up, I was left with a dilemma: ask Mom for the money (anywhere from twenty-five cents to a dollar) and break the family rule, or miss out on the social event of the week. I recall that I most often had twenty-five to thirty-five cents to spend and hoped that my friends with more expansive budgets would share their french fries with me. I learned quickly who cared enough to notice and share; that lesson in kindness has stuck with me.

Despite our financial strain, we were rich in the ways that mattered most. I was about seven years old, playing in my front yard, when someone from my new school walked by. The young girl, who had previously only seen me in my Catholic schoolgirl uniform, glanced at my house—paint chipping, front stairs collapsing. She looked me squarely in the eyes and in a somewhat unforgiving tone, she said, "Do you live *here*?!"

"Yes," I responded.

"Ohhh," she said, "I used to think you were rich!"

I ran directly to Mom. She was methodically ironing her white nurse's uniform and seemed unfazed when I ran into the room crying.

Mom turned toward me and calmly said, "Shelly, you have all of these brothers and sisters and so very much love. *You are rich.* Don't ever forget that."

I instantly stopped crying and returned to playing. I knew she was right, and I knew that she was the foundation of so much of the love I had experienced. I was reminded that love, above all else, is what matters most. I knew I would be called upon to carry that message forward. That day and that conversation left an imprint on my soul;

that love would guide me as I created and raised my new family.

I have a large, loving family. I *am* rich. I am the *sister* to Brian, Kathleen, Maureen, Dan, Mary Lou, Margaret Ann, Francis, Patrick, Tim, Loretta, Jean, Nancy, Tom, and Mary Ellen. In my freshman year of college, it was not unusual for my friends to ask me to rattle off these names in a rapid fire manner. It took me about fifteen seconds or so, the faster the better and more impressive for my friends! They were amazed at the list of characters, but it was easy for me, as they were all close to my heart. They are all unique and distinct individuals, and I love each and every one of them.

I have fond and fun memories of and with each of my siblings stretching all the way back to Grace Avenue. I recall Brian, studying in his room, asking—no, pleading—for us to be quiet. I can still picture Kathleen ("Queenie," as we lovingly called her) tightly gripping her list as she assigned each of us a house chore. She did her best to keep us in line; she also kept us together—a tall order. Kath and her husband Dale have now hosted the McNamara Christmas Party for almost forty years. Maureen, I can still see her smiling in her freshly earned nurse's cap, proud to follow Mom's path as she was officially welcomed in as a health care professional. Dan, always smiling, always greeted me with a heartfelt question: "How are you, Shell?" In later years, his greeting evolved to, "How are your girls, Shell? They are such beautiful kids." Mary Lou, one of my second moms, always made me feel loved—deeply loved. She and her husband Bob took us to McDonald's for burgers and fries, and occasionally a milkshake if the budget allowed.

Margaret Ann was the official caregiver for Tom and me when she was in high school, rushing home each day to get there before Mom left for work at 2:30 pm. She used her own money to buy us our first bicycles. A generous heart. Fran, always working at one of his many jobs so he could contribute to our stretched household budget, bought me my first pair of ice skates. They were white and like gold to me. Patrick, our high school and college football player, paid me twenty-five cents a week to make and pack his daily lunch—three egg salad sandwiches. Never missed a payment. Tim, the kind of guy who would give you his last dollar if you needed it, often treated the neighborhood kids to a trip to Dairy Isle for ice cream cones. I remember when he broke his leg jumping from the top of the local movie theatre building. Kind heart, with crazy ideas sometimes.

Loretta, I remember the laughter that seemed to follow her everywhere. I wore her striped turtleneck for my school picture. I think that sweater can be found in the school photo for two or three of us sisters; nice clothes were hard to come by in our home. Jean, with her rare, calm presence in our crazy home, has always looked out for me. She still refers to me as "my little sister, Shelly," which makes me smile. Nancy purchased her first stereo system in high school with the money she earned working at McDonald's. She introduced me to music and trusted me with her sacred stereo system. I spent countless hours listening to her music: Diana Ross, Jim Croce, The Eagles, and Earth, Wind & Fire.

Tom played sports year-round and invited me to every game. Mom bought us both a summer pass for the nearby public swimming pool at Madison Park. She included swimming lessons. I assumed it was a gift granted to all of us, but sometime in my forties, I learned that we were the only two kids in the family who'd had this privilege. It's often true that those with privilege don't notice that others are lacking.

Mary Ellen, who lived only three months, went on to be an angel for all of us.

Thanks to my siblings, I am an *aunt* now—"Aunt Shell"—to thirty-eight nieces and nephews and more than seventy-five great nieces and nephews. Our family continues to grow in both numbers and love.

With my wife Cindy, I am a *mother* to . . .

Ali, a creative, optimistic problem solver with a deep love for nature and passion for the environment.

Kate, who is smart, kind, and driven to make a meaningful difference in the world. She is both insightful and funny.

Nicole, our spontaneous and playful daughter. Smart. Fun. Always questioning why and why not. She sees possibilities in everything and everyone.

I also have the privilege of having a "little man," Casey, in my life. He is the man of the family. Our canine companion. In the words of my daughters, I treat him more like a human than a dog!

Our children have given us so many gifts over the years. The gift of joy has been one of them. I'll never forget when Ali, at the age of three, stepped out of her time-out chair to say to me, "Mommy, I finally figured it out—you're the problem!" Or another day when she was in time out and asked the infamous question every child wants to ask their parent at some point or another: "Mommy—who made you the boss of me?!" (I told her it was God.) When Kate introduced herself to the new babysitter: "Hi, I'm Kate. I have two sisters, two mommies, and no daddy." Then there was the time she ran into the room, a little stressed and panicked: "I need a mommy—any mommy—either mommy—I just need a mommy." (Don't we all?!) When we moved into a new house in Connecticut and Nicole, just five years old, asked, "Hey . . . are we like the only family in the world with two moms or what?!" Or at the age of four, when she said, "You know what I want? I want you two to get married so I can clap—and clap and clap . . ." This child, those words, foreshadowed such a treasured day for our family, the day that I would be legally wed.

In 2014, I became a *wife* to my life partner, Cindy. She is creative. Funny. Super smart. Kind—so very kind. The most caring, loving, gentle soul you will ever meet. She is home to me.

I am a *storyteller*. I write and tell stories to open hearts and minds and to heal from the struggles of my own journey. This is a core component of who I am, an identity closely linked to the values of love and inclusion. I write about love, loss, the power of healing, and the many things we do to create distance and divide from each other. My "differentness," which has caused me to be minimized and sidelined, has also revealed the transformative nature of compassion and empathy to me. I have immense empathy for those left behind or left out, and I want my story and storytelling to help heal the pain that exists within and between people.

I am also an *"out" business leader and corporate executive* at Procter & Gamble, one of the world's largest consumer goods companies. Human resources is my chosen profession, which I discovered while taking an organizational psychology class at the University of Michigan. I read about organization development, a field of study focused on developing individuals, teams, and organizations with a values-based, humanistic approach. I had finally discovered a profession that deeply connected me, my work, and my passion for growth. I loved my experience at U of M, and I love the profession and purpose I discovered there. In my late twenties, I received a Master of Science degree in Organization Development from Case Western Reserve University. I learned from and with some outstanding teachers and students.

Since joining P&G in 1985, I have had many assignments and experiences that have helped me grow, and along the way, I have helped others grow. In particular, through visiting nearly twenty-five countries and working for a global corporation, I have learned from and collaborated with an extremely diverse range of people. These relationships around the world have helped me grow as a human being and as a human resources professional.

My thirty-plus years in business have taught me that great leaders and caring human beings value, respect, and include others. They don't allow people to be treated as "less than." They know that creating space and support for the full range of humanity drives innovation and growth. The data supports this statement. Organizations with cultures of inclusivity are twice as likely to meet or exceed their financial targets, and they are six times more likely to be innovative.[1]

When people sit along the edges, treated as "less than," we miss . . .

. . . their wisdom and insight

. . . relationships

. . . the impact they can have on our lives, organizations and communities.

At my company, we rely on empathy and human connection to lead us as we innovate for our diverse consumer base. Within our company, we value and proactively seek to build and nurture a diverse workforce. An investment in inclusion is a human choice and a business choice. It's the key to creating products that truly serve the world's consumers. Inclusion supports expansion and growth. At P&G, we respect and include because it's the right thing to do and because it enables us to grow our business.

Sadly, there are people all around us who have been made to feel "less than." I have been made to feel less than. Most of us in the LGBTQ+ community have experienced a level of rejection or judgment that left us with deep emotional wounds. And each day, thousands of teenagers ask themselves if life is worth living.

Teen suicide is a major issue in our country, with more than 3,000

---

high school-aged kids attempting suicide, on average, each day.[2] Lesbian, gay, and bisexual youth are almost five times more likely to attempt suicide than heterosexual youth.[3] These are human beings in need of support and the chance to live full lives. It saddens me to know that for some of these young people, the lack of support they needed was a contributing factor. I feel compelled to educate adults—corporate executives and parents—about what they can do to be more proactively supportive. I want us all to understand the cost of exclusion; it is high.

The fear of consequences, both personal and professional, is real. We need to critically think about the words we use to talk about people who are different than us—to listen to our words and the effect we attach to them when we speak about people who are lesbian, gay, bisexual, or transgender. Hateful words create harm and shame. I want all children and human beings to feel valued and supported—without condition.

At the core, I believe that we have an obligation and responsibility to do something, to reach out, value, respect, and include all. I have felt and experienced the deep and endless power of love. Now, I no longer regret or apologize for who I am or how I am. It hasn't always been that way. Today, I use the insight I have gained to build connections and community with others, and I encourage you to do the same.

The fact that I am a lesbian has given me some unique, deep insights. I know the feeling of inclusion and privilege, and I know the pain of judgment and exclusion. I invite you to listen and learn from the stories and poems I share. My intent is to bring more compassion

---

2 The Jason Foundation: http://prp.jasonfoundation.com/facts/youth-suicide-statistics/

3 The Trevor Project: https://www.thetrevorproject.org/resources/preventing-suicide/facts-about-suicide/#sm.0000henelns7ldhry5t1oj1xjmaan

and love into the world. I wish for each of us to identify what we can individually do to bring about more love and respect for all.

What aspects of your childhood shaped who you are and how you operate in the world?

Who do you treat as "less than?"

Who do you know that sits outside the circle of privilege?

How can you make them feel included?

Where can you be more loving? More giving?

2. Compelled to Write, Driven to Speak

Maybe it's in the loss that I've learned to give.

My writing began as a way to process pain. When I was sixteen years old, my sister Loretta's best friend was killed by a drunk driver. Mary Ann was only twenty-three years old when she died. I remember the phone call. I remember the feelings of panic and pain. I remember sitting on the couch next to Loretta. A few of my siblings walked in and out of the room, not knowing what to do. I stayed with my sister. She lay on the couch, screaming and crying aloud. I sat at the end of the couch. I couldn't leave her. I stayed there for a long while. I am not sure that she even knew I was there. I stayed to comfort her. I stayed to find comfort for myself. This loss felt like more than either of us could bear.

At some point during those days or weeks after Mary Ann's death, I went on a really long walk with Chris, Mary Ann's brother and my close childhood friend. We talked. We cried. We hugged each other as if we could hold on tightly enough that maybe this connection could bring her back to earth. The loss of Mary Ann was more than we could truly process, but we consoled each other. I remember that walk and that hug. I also recall the deep sadness I had for Chris and the feelings of guilt knowing that I would go home that day and see my sister.

Mary Ann was one of the many teenagers and young adults that frequently came to my childhood home. But Mary Ann was special to me. She sat with me. She talked with me. I recall most that she listened to my stories. I was a talkative child. I loved to tell stories, and she listened to me. She was that rare person who enjoyed just "being" with you. She became like another older sister to me. She wasn't just my sister's best friend; she was a dear friend to our whole family. She was my dear friend Chris's older sister. Her death deeply affected me.

As my family preferred laughter over pain, I didn't have an outlet to deal with the grief. Thus, I sat and wrote my first poem. This was the beginning of my writing journey.

Or So They Say

The wind was blowing—the leaves falling
Another hour, another day
Another life—and who's to blame?
The night was ceasing—God was calling
He watches us all—or so they say

The factor was timing—the driver was drinking
A door opened, a door closed
The life was hers—and why not his?
The sirens were ringing—people were crying
He always keeps order—or so they say

My life was growing—hers was going
If only then, if only now
Why not me—and why not you?
The questions were coming—answers were lacking
He has his reasons—or so they say

Still we are living—but not understanding
No longer questioning—but rather accepting
It was her time—her own special time

We have all grown—we have all changed
By having known her, loved her, and lost her

I was born in April 1963, just thirteen months after my sister Mary Ellen (another Mary) was born in March 1962. Some would refer to us as Irish twins, given the short time span between our births. Mary Ellen was born with Down syndrome and a hole in her heart. After living on this Earth for a mere three months, she passed away in June of 1962, devastating my mother and my siblings. I heard a few stories of Mary Ellen's birth and death throughout my life, but they were brief and rare. My family avoided painful topics; we had enough to struggle with on a daily basis. We didn't have the capacity to take on any more.

I don't remember exactly when my anxiety began, I just know I felt anxious from a very young age. I would anxiously wait for my mom to come home from work on weekend nights. I was anxious on Sunday nights, knowing that Mom was going back to work on Monday. I anxiously waited for my report card, hoping I got straight As. And I vividly remember being anxious about being left alone in my house; our home had a constant level of chaos until those evenings when everyone seemed to suddenly disappear into their individual social lives. I thought the feeling of anxiety was a normal state. It was years later I learned that while it was *my* normal state, it was certainly not an *acceptable* normal state.

By my late twenties, I had developed a deep and specific anxiety. My anxiety was rooted in a fear that family, friends, and work colleagues would find out that I was gay. I was very selective, sharing the fact that I was gay with few people. My fear was well-founded—the culture around me and the narratives I heard throughout the '80s and early '90s were very homophobic. This fear drove me to singularly pursue external validation as a sort of distraction, or maybe a form of insurance that would guarantee others' love for me even after they discovered this aspect of my identity. Running from myself and taking energy to hide a core part of my identity cost me greatly.

When I was in my early thirties, I was going through a very difficult personal time. I was experiencing profound levels of anxiety. I was deeply suffering from the lack of congruency I felt. With the help of a professional counselor, I came to realize that I had built a life and identity that was oriented "from the outside in." I focused my energy on doing things that would get me accolades and appreciation from others—academic success, professional progress, and achievement. I built walls that prevented people from really seeing me or getting too close. If someone got close, I just might lose them. It took many years of therapy for me to realize the only way for me to have authentic, deep connections to other human beings was by being myself. This would require me to first accept and love myself—accolades and accomplishments set aside.

I yearned for the peace that comes only when you love yourself first. I yearned to live "from the inside out." But I needed to dive in a bit deeper to discover what motivated me. In my solitude, I questioned: Who am I? What does come from the inside out?

One night, I had a dream about my deceased sister Mary Ellen. It was a very clear dream. She seemed very real, and so was her message to me that *all love starts with self-love*. It was a dream that left me with a lingering feeling and insight.

I was working deeply on myself. With the help of therapy, self-reflection, and maturity, I went from living in a near constant state of anxiety with intermittent panic attacks, to a place of peace. I had been working with a counselor for some time, but it was this event that became the tipping point to get me back to center. It would be more than fifteen years before I would have another panic attack. My sense of purpose, my clarity for what would bring me joy, and my passion for writing were only growing with each day. Cindy and

I had our first child a few years later.

Mary Ellen reminded me that we can never truly love another until we love ourselves. That dream made it clear that my purpose was to open hearts and minds and build connections that help heal the world. I just never anticipated how deeply important this work would become. I didn't know that the key to unlocking my joy and peace was resting inside me all those many years.

Both Mary Ann and Mary Ellen gave me the motivation to *write*.

It was my nephew, Kevin McCarthy, who gave me the courage to *speak*.

Kevin was born in May 1983. I was twenty years old at the time, away at college, and had just recently fallen in love with Cindy. Kevin and I were separated in distance, time, and life stage, but we always felt connected—deeply connected. Could it have been that he was one of the cutest little kids I had ever seen? Maybe. He was awfully cute. Was it that he was the youngest grandchild of Grandma Mac for three whole years (a record for the McNamara family!)? Maybe. I did spend a lot of time with Kevin in my mother's home. He visited frequently and entertained us all with his dancing, music, and playful spirit. He brought out a unique joy in my mother that I loved witnessing. My mother would laugh loudly and smile brightly as she watched this little Irish boy engage the world with his uniqueness. He melted her heart and, in turn, mine.

As he matured, Kevin and I had deeper and more meaningful conversations. We both cared for and about people. We both despised injustice and hate and felt called to do work that eliminated them. We had a special connection that I miss each day.

Kevin was with us such a short time on this Earth. At the age of seventeen, Kevin contracted meningitis and nearly died. The meningitis caused encephalitis, a swelling of the brain, and this left him with many challenges. Kevin lived another ten years, but the last few years of his life were extremely difficult for him and his family. We all hated seeing him suffer.

Kevin passed away in 2010 at the age of twenty-seven, and my life was forever changed. In my journey of grief, I eventually realized that Kevin's passing created an opening and a rebirth in me and in my life.

Why tell you about Kevin? Kevin was my inspiration and motivation to publicly share the hundreds of stories I have written over the years, and that sharing has made a difference for many people. By telling my story so publicly, and with such raw honesty and vulnerability, I have discovered and experienced a deep connection with others—many of whom I would never have met along my journey. We have helped each other become stronger, more accepting, and more loving human beings. I had always known that my poetry and stories were meant for a broader audience, but it was the depth of my grief and the contemplative silence of Kevin's death that created the opening. I was motivated to do more good in the world—in his honor.

Kevin was a model of kindness and courage; he showed love for all, without exception. It came naturally to him. I work at it every day. He was my inspiration to share, to use the words I have been given to open hearts and minds, to build connections between human beings, not more distance. We all need inspiration. We all need more connection.

My grief for Kevin's loss has not gone; today, it rests in my heart and hurts deeply. I cry when I hear Irish music; sometimes I think I hear his voice or his laugh, only to turn around and see a different young man in front of me. Grief takes time. I find the depth of my pain remains constant—it's a deep hole. The duration of the feeling is less; the pain passes more quickly as time moves on. The love never fades. Kevin taught me to love self and others more deeply, more authentically. It's this gift I hold on to most closely.

It was important for me to honor Kevin at his funeral services and in the life I live each day. We all need a Kevin in our lives.

Kevin's Funeral, St. Colman Church, Cleveland, Ohio –
July 24, 2010
Excerpts from the Eulogy by Shelly McNamara

It is an honor and privilege to share the insights, experiences, and stories about Kevin from his family and friends . . .

Kevin had the unique ability to make everyone feel special, and he gave love just by being. He was driven by a deep sense of fairness and justice, which was rooted in his deep respect and compassion for all. He was always on the side of those he saw as disadvantaged in the realms of power and privilege.

Kevin taught us all much about love—he gave it without conditions.

He taught us about courage and grace—he never complained about his challenging health condition.

Kevin, dear Kevin, rest in peace. Go knowing that you left a deep imprint on our hearts and souls that will last forever. Go with our love. Kevin, I loved you like a son. I will miss you. Because of you, though, I will slow down. I will smell more flowers and listen more intently to the music. I will play and laugh more with the kids, and love more deeply. We will all care for and about the family you love so dearly. We will find some peace knowing that you are laughing with your grandparents and Uncle Brian, drinking your first beer in five years with all of your Irish relatives, and that you are only a thought away. It is only a moment until we are together again.

I wrote you a poem . . .

Until Then

We will always remember . . .
Your face—handsome and angelic
Your smile—innocent, yet deeply knowing
Your kindness—you gave just by being
Your tin whistle & fiddle—you lightened our spirits
Your contagious Irish laugh
Your heart—you loved us and we loved you
Your gentle loving spirit

You are a child of God
Now in the arms of the Lord
Rest in His peace
Rest in His love

It's only a moment until we are together again . . .
Until then, we will remember . . .
I love you, Kevin.
Aunt Shelly

I Learned

Maybe it's in the loss
That I've learned to give

From rejection
I learned to embrace

In the judgment
I learned to accept

In the dishonor
I learned to love and honor all

In the end
I learned to love you and me

Mary Ann's sudden death opened the passageway to my heart and my gift of poetry. I'm grateful for Mary Ann and the gift I received.

Mary Ellen's absence seemed to hang over our family in unspoken ways that no one wanted to discuss. I am grateful for the healing connection I had with her; the transformative dream became a major turning point and tipping point in my journey of self-discovery and healing.

Kevin's life and passing forever changed me. He was an angel on earth for me. I smiled a lot in his presence, while also feeling the deepest sense of calmness and peace. And I felt loved, always. The loss of his physical presence left me deeply wounded and deeply driven to do the work I had always known I was called to do. The written word and storytelling became core to who I am.

How do you process pain?

What have you learned from the losses in your life?

Who were the ones to trigger you to live the life you were meant to live?

What do you feel called to do?

3. Regret & Redemption

Do you need me to forgive and say goodbye? Or do I?

I am the daughter of a man who lived a lifetime of regret.

Bernard McNamara was what I would call a casualty of World War II. He flew B-1 bomber jets. To cope with the stress of war, he and his fellow soldiers habitually lined shots of alcohol up in a row on the table upon returning from their missions. They drank to dull the pain of war. Like some who fought in that war, he came home addicted.

My father drank a lot. He drank away from our home just as often as he did in it. Yet it didn't seem to matter where he drank—our home would nevertheless serve as the principal outlet for his anger. Though I did not witness his angry outbursts like my older siblings, I did hear their stories. They talked about his anger, his rage, and his incessant absence. He physically pushed and shoved any of his children that got in between him and his target of anger (our mother), or his drink of choice (beer or whiskey).

As his alcoholism progressed, his time away from our home increased. During his final year of living in our home, it became clear that he had started a relationship with another woman. I have memories of her calling our home. In those days, the phone hung on the wall in a central place, which meant answering it was visible and noticed by all. One of my sisters would answer the phone and quickly hang up upon realizing who it was. I don't have clarity as to why this woman repeatedly called our house. We were young, and though we could not understand the complexity of the situation, this seemed like such an overt invasion of our home. Furthermore, it was evidence of my father actively fostering his connections with people outside my family when he made no efforts to do so within our home. The desire for him to leave our home only grew.

I remember this childhood home so very clearly. There were three entrances to the house—front, back, and side. The side door connected you to four stairs that led to the kitchen. It was easy to go unnoticed when you entered this door. It was distant and separate from the busy parts of the home, the living and family rooms.

It was through this door—the side door—that my father entered in 1967. It was a suitable entry point; it was distant and separate, like him. I was just four years old, and my brother Tom was six. We both ran to greet him. I gave him a big hug. I remember that. In contrast, Mom sat anxiously waiting in the living room, alone. The rest of my siblings seemed to vanish minutes before his arrival. Tom and I were young and naive. We didn't carry the fear and anger that defined our siblings' daily lives. For me and Tom, our innocence remained. Our father had been gone for what seemed to me like weeks or months, but this would be his last visit to our home on Grace Avenue. This was the last time I would hug my father for seventeen years.

I'd like to say that there was anger or disappointment about his leaving, but there wasn't. In fact, the feeling I recall most present in our home was relief. Relief that this abusive, raging alcoholic had walked out. Leaving us was the best choice he could have made, and I am glad he made it.

I saw my father briefly one day in the late '70s. Someone in my family heard that our father was working at a retail store on the other side of town. Motivated by curiosity and steeped in teenage spontaneity, my brother Tom and I drove there with the hope that we would see our father. We never thought about or talked about what we would actually do or say if we did indeed meet him.

As fate would have it, the moment we walked through the door, he was directly in front of us. Although I recognized my father, I saw a man in front of me that I did not know. I'd expected to have deep feelings of connection or loss; I actually felt confused and disoriented. I wanted him to recognize us and say something meaningful, deep. Instead, he asked if we had any questions about the merchandise.

We didn't introduce ourselves or acknowledge who he was, but I'm certain he recognized us. We hadn't changed that much in twelve years. In his silence, he denied our relationship. He lacked the courage to face us and move beyond his own shame. Tom asked a random question, and we quickly left the store. We were strangers with a connection that none of us were capable of actualizing, at least not in that moment.

I would next see my father in 1984. He was gambling at the racetrack in Cleveland, Ohio, where he had a massive heart attack. On that day, the Catholic priest gave him his last rites, believing he was transitioning to the other side. My brothers and sisters went to his bedside to see him, but I was hundreds of miles away at college and could not make it to the hospital.

As it turned out, this was not his day to die. His life though, was crumbling and nearing the end. Weeks later, I came home from school to see him. I was twenty-one years old at the time. As I walked into my sister's living room where my father was sitting, I felt as though I was meeting him for the first time. We had no history, or at least none that I could recall. I was an adult, with years of life and experiences that defined me. He did not know me, and I also understood that I didn't really know him. To me, he was "the mystery man." I stood before him, trying to make sense of that day and all of the years that had passed since that final visit to Grace Avenue. I looked into his eyes and felt the depth of my mother's pain caused by his absence and his alcoholism. And so, I wrote . . .

The Mystery Man

Now, seeing the mystery man
Hardly mentioned, spoken, or heard of
The mythical man not to be seen

Today, here and now, looking into your saddened eyes
Pain wells up inside me—I dare to breathe

To recreate a past of twenty years
To tell you of the thousand times I asked myself—why?

Now, I see the pain and the tears
Held so tightly within this God-sent woman—my mother

How to view, name, or call one a father?

I had questions I yearned to ask him, but in the wake of his frailty and immense vulnerability, these went unspoken.

Yet, I still could not overcome the certain persistence of resentment I felt, which had built up over the years. I knew that he wasn't deserving of the title "father." His absence made this name meaningless and disconnected. I would not grant him that title; he had not earned that privilege. He left his wife, my loving, God-sent mother, Helen. He abandoned his fifteen children, fourteen of us living when he officially left our home.

Mary Ellen passed away just a few years before my father's departure. I have often thought that Mary Ellen left because the pain in our family was too much to bear. That hole in her heart came to symbolize the deep pain in my family caused by a father who chose a drink over his family, and then the exit door instead of facing his illness and his responsibilities. The gaping hole he left in our family was real—palpable. It was a hole that was, in large part, created by the damage done by his drinking and the subsequent presence of despair and fear in our household, less by his absence. He left his children and wife to process and heal on our own.

In this moment, this resentment and pain weighed on me. Yet, as I looked into the eyes of this mystery man now as a young adult, I wondered . . . is it time to forgive? And so, I wrote . . .

Is it Time to Forgive?

How do you say goodbye
To someone you never knew
Never saw
Never loved

How do you forgive someone
Who never apologized
For the pain
The suffering
The absence

How do you learn
To trust again

Once they walk out on you
The pain stays
Trust impossible to find

Dear father, you left a void
A chasm no one could ever fill

Do you need me to forgive and say goodbye?
Or do I?

I stayed connected with my father for about a year after his event at the racetrack. We exchanged a few letters (through the US postal service!), a few, brief visits, and one phone conversation. His reemergence into our family system caused strain. A few felt strongly about helping him to heal. Others, with fresh memories of his anger, violence, and absence, kept their distance. Both of these choices were understandable and valid. I chose to stay connected, though in a limited capacity, and on the condition that he abstain from alcohol.

His abstinence lasted about nine months—not very long, and not long enough. And after he began drinking again, he also stopped taking his medications. At that point, he knew that he had ruined his last chance for redemption in the eyes of his children. This seemed to be when he "gave up" and finally gave in to his illness—alcoholism. In that year, his final year on Earth, I didn't find answers. He didn't find peace. We didn't recreate our family or fill the void left by his many years of absence.

My father passed away in May 1986.

When he passed away, I was sad, more for what we never had than what we had and lost. We never had the chance to experience life together, so he remained a mystery man to me. I remained distant and unknown to him.

Yet, I learned from this experience and his life. As a witness to his tumultuous relationship with our family and with alcohol, I learned about the importance of choice. Each and every day provides us the opportunity to choose differently and begin again. We only need to exercise that choice, as no one can do it for us. I learned about the value of commitment and strength in the face of adversity—my mother was deeply committed to the health and well-being of her fifteen children. She never gave up on us or on being a mother. She modeled a strength of character and resilience that my father lacked.

I do wonder, was my father a victim of World War II? A victim of his own weakness, his decision to drink each day? A victim of a society and culture that lacked the insight for how to treat alcoholism? All possibilities, overlapping and intersecting causes. I know that alcoholism creates generations of loss. I am still discovering the full impact on me and our broader family.

Following my father's death, I discovered a poem that he had written. Considering my passion for writing, we may have been connected in ways I couldn't understand. He wrote . . .

Hope (by Bernard McNamara)

The leaves will soon be
On the trees outside my window

The snow in the background
Does not change my view

Of belief in a Hope of Springtime
And Hope of Springtime Change

A Hope and Prayer for forgiveness
From all the people I have hurt
Without intent

Now with hope Spring is here
Soon I hope

His poem gave me some peace and eroded a bit of my resentment. He'd known the pain he caused. He'd wanted forgiveness, and he had not given up hope.

For my mother, pain of any kind was too much to cling to for long. She forgave my father in her gracious, loving way—without fanfare, and with few words. Her public show of forgiveness was brief, but deeply meaningful.

It was Christmas Day, 1986, seven months after my father's passing. We were all gathered at Mom's house for Christmas dinner. Christmas morning and afternoon were open for celebrating with in-laws, but Christmas dinner was dedicated time for Mom, her fourteen children, and their respective families. Mom, known as "Grandma Mac" to her then-thirty (now forty-one) grandchildren always created an atmosphere of laughter and love. We treasured Christmas night. Included in the celebration was a scrumptious turkey dinner, a game of charades, and a gift exchange.

We began our annual gift giving ritual with all of the grandchildren gathered together on Grandma Mac's living room floor. It was important to my mother that no matter how small or modest the gifts were, she gave one to each and every one of her grandchildren. I helped her buy, organize, and wrap the gifts. On Christmas evening, I was her little elf, handing her each gift and whispering, "This one is for . . ." as the pile of gifts dwindled.

I loved seeing the joy she took in giving. She would say to me, "It's the thought that counts, Shelly. I want each of these kids to know that I thought of them." I handed her one gift at a time—she called out the name. The roll call was long! A playful, joyful ritual.

On this Christmas evening, something unexpected happened. Once the last grandchild received their gift, Mom said, "Okay, now I want all fourteen of my kids to come in here."

I was Mom's official "gift wrapper," and I didn't recognize the stack she was now carrying.

She continued, "Okay, is everyone here? I want you all to open this gift at the same time."

Amidst some nervous laughter, I was anxious, yet intrigued.

The sound of crinkling wrapping paper filled the air. I tore away the paper, and there he was, staring right at me—my father, our father. Mom had framed Dad's military photo for each of us. He looked so very professional and handsome. He was so very handsome.

More nervous laughter, darting eyes, and a bit of confusion filled the air.

She finally spoke: "Well, he *is* your father, you know."

That was it. She didn't say anything more. The silence shifted to lots of chatter: "Who is that? Why did Grandma give you that?" A few tears, a few nervous laughs, and a few awkward smiles.

In our family, we avoided sadness and conflict—these were emotions that seemed too difficult to feel or process. Some tell me that is part of our inherited Irish culture, others may say it was a survival mechanism that resulted from our challenging circumstances. I struggled to reconcile the fact that amidst my grief, I felt an underlying sense of relief that my mother forgave her husband, our father, so publicly and personally. A burden released. In her way, in this moment of healing, she was inviting all of her children to do the same.

Soon enough, I would truly forgive my father, and I hoped that my brothers and sisters did the same. I forgave because the hurt was too difficult to carry. I forgave because I saw the deep regret in his eyes and in his written word. I forgave because I didn't want the rage and anger to live on in another generation. I forgave because I didn't want to risk choosing alcohol as a way to numb anger. Only then could I feel the peace and calm that comes with forgiveness.

I also hope that my father forgave himself for leaving the family he created, for choosing a drink over lasting relationships. I hope for him that he learned, forgave, and left this earth with some peace. He taught me how I didn't want my life to be. I would choose better. I would be free and live free. I would love and be loved. I would not run away from myself or others. I would not live a life of regret. I would not walk by my own dreams, or walk past those I love.

I did get to see what regret looked like and felt like from the receiving end. I realized, though, that I had not been abandoned. So often, the story of regret is followed by a story of redemption; mine was no different. My mother had redeemed him. She was an extraordinary mother. She sewed deep love and laughter into our hearts and lives and modeled a strength of character and resilience that my father lacked. My brothers and sisters also stepped in to redeem their father and provide unconditional love and support for me, their baby sister. It was important for me to honor them, and so I wrote . . .

Dear Brother – Dear Sister

Thank you for stepping in
For giving love
And safety

No one could know
The pain
The void
The loss

Felt only when
A parent walks
Out on you

The pain is too much
The void is too deep

There is never goodbye for us

I love you
Forever

We live our lives one moment at a time, one decision at a time. We risk. At times, we trip. We fall. We learn. In the journey of being human, we learn the power of forgiveness from both sides.

And sometimes, we realize that the only way to begin again is to forgive.

Is there someone you need to forgive? Or do you need to ask for forgiveness?

Do you have hope for a change in your life? What can you do to initiate this change?

Has addiction affected your life or the lives of your loved ones? Is there room or opportunity for progress, better health, or healing?

4. Love More. Judge Less.

I wish that I had loved more, and judged less.

Regret over what has been said or done, regret over what hasn't been said or done—or regret over something that just wasn't resolved—can eat away at you for a long time.

My eldest brother, Brian, and I came close to the doorstep of regret in our relationship, but didn't walk through that door.

The relationship I had with Brian is most easily described in a few words:

Respect: We both found a way to finance our undergraduate and graduate degrees. This took persistence, commitment, and hard work, given our challenging family situation and economic status. He found a way to become a doctor—a life dream for him and my mother. In my first year of work post undergraduate school, every time he saw me, he would ask, "So, are you a vice president yet?" My response: "Nope. Not yet. And likely not ever." I truly didn't see that as an option or likely outcome for me. He knew better.

Laughter: My brother was funny, so very funny. He made me laugh, especially when he chided our mother with the sole purpose of making her smile. I loved watching the joy that he brought to her.

Love: We had mutual respect, and maybe even a bit of admiration for the journey we had each traversed. This formed the basis of a deep love for each other.

Distance: We were a generation apart; Brian was nearly twenty years older than me. There was a big gap in our life stages, life interests, and life struggles. My brother wasn't the best at emotional human connection. I know he carried pain from my father's impact—potentially holding pain and anger from which he had not healed. I know now that back then, I created distance to avoid potential judgment.

It was this distance in emotional connection that I felt more often than not. We laughed together, we discussed current events and topics, and we both worked to make Mom smile and laugh, often bantering back and forth. Yet, we avoided uncomfortable topics. Brian was kind to Cindy and engaged with both of us when he saw us (usually at Mom's house), but he kept his conversations fairly safe and surface. In hindsight, I believe that I created that norm—I wasn't fully "out" then, and I created distance to keep safe. I don't blame either of us for the distance, but I do recall what it felt like then, and I know exactly when and how that distance and gap disappeared—and it happened just in time.

It's rare to know when our "last time" with each other will be. Yet, on some unspoken level, I believe my brother and I knew on the last two occasions we saw each other. The last two conversations we had were deeply meaningful to me and for our relationship.

Nine months before Brian's death, in July of 1997, Cindy was pregnant with our eldest daughter, Ali. We attended a few of the typical McNamara family events—dinner at a restaurant and a picnic in the park. We had experienced a range of reactions from my family members upon sharing the news of our emerging new status as parents, but mostly support. Brian was silent on the topic. In fact, he seemed to keep more of a distance from us. I did know that my brother loved me, but I always felt that he struggled with beliefs he had inherited from family and religion that minimized us and somehow painted us as "less worthy" of being parents.

Violating the norms of our family and our relationship, I initiated a difficult conversation with my brother: "I want you to be happy for us. We are going to be parents soon, and we are so very excited about that. I really hope you can be happy for us."

I saw a shift in him. The shifts I witnessed were subtle, not monumental. They were important, and they were timely. My instinct tells me that it was a part of a broader moment of transformation for him, from which I benefited. He was surprised by my directness. He listened. He internalized what I was saying. Brian seemed to "soften." He talked with both of us more that evening, and he seemed more at ease with us and likely our impending parenthood.

Ali was born a few months later, in October 1997. We traveled to Cleveland in December to celebrate Christmas and our new baby. Having Ali and holding her triggered a unique love known and felt only by a parent. I was "home" when I held this baby, and anxious to share that love we felt.

In the midst of our Christmas party, I stumbled upon Brian sitting alone in a room. This is an incredible feat, to find a moment and a location to be alone at a McNamara family gathering.

Brian called me over to him and said, "Your daughter is beautiful, just beautiful."

He smiled as he spoke. His eyes twinkled in ways they never had before. If any judgment had been there, it was now replaced by love. No labels, simply love. Just then, Cindy came into the room and snapped our picture.

That was the last conversation I had with my brother, Brian. That photograph was the last photo I had of him.

The moment that everything changed, I was at work, leading a discussion with my manager and an HR vice president. My assistant,

Kim, came to the door to interrupt us. She whispered something to my manager. I sensed that the message was for me and instinctively knew that whatever had happened or was happening wasn't good.

Someone asked me to call Cindy: "She needs to talk to you right away. She said to tell you that Ali (who was just six months old) is fine."

I don't remember how I got back to my office, but I do remember every word that Cindy spoke to me: "Shelly, you need to come home. Your brother Brian had a heart attack while at work. They tried to save him. He was with a patient in the emergency room, went to his desk, and never returned. His nurse found him dead at his desk. There was a Code Blue, and they tried for over an hour to revive him. I am so sorry, but he passed away. All of your brothers and sisters made it to the hospital."

The only words I could muster up were, "Please tell me NO—this didn't happen. Oh my God, NO. Cindy, I'm on my way home. Get Ali ready to drive to Cleveland."

In April 1998, my brother Brian—Doctor Brian Joseph Mc-Namara—had passed away in his own emergency room, the place where he saved countless lives but couldn't be saved. A Code Blue rang loudly throughout the hospital, including in my sister Margaret's ears while she worked just a few corridors away. She would later tell us that she had a bad feeling when this Code Blue rang out. She wasn't surprised when a fellow staff member came to escort her to the ER. She, like all of my siblings, had the chance to say goodbye to our brother Brian in the emergency room, in his emergency room. His colleagues allowed for the family to pay their respects and say goodbye before my brother left his ER for his transition to heaven.

Brian left behind no regrets in our relationship, only love. Any limits or labels that may have previously held him or me back were long gone, replaced by love. He looked so peaceful to me in what became my final moments on earth with him in December of 1997.

Blinded

What will it take for you to
See me as I am

To see the gifts I have been given
Just as you and yours

We miss each other
We walk past
We overlook

We never see
What each of us really has or is

Blinded by our notion of
What or who we should be

Brian was a wonderful man who I felt compelled to honor. He was an amazing father and husband. He was an outstanding physician. How do I know this? Every EMT, firefighter, nurse, doctor, and lab technician that came to pay their respects told me.

In the Catholic tradition, we had a wake, a showing of the body in a casket with family standing nearby to greet the mourners, the extended family and friends who came to pay their respects and say their goodbyes. My siblings and I stood in line with Brian's family, greeting and consoling people for close to twelve hours. My brother was respected and adored. His wife, Carol, and their six children were loved. Hundreds and hundreds of people showed up to support and love them. This was only our first loss in 1998, as Mom passed away from Alzheimer's eight months later.

Who was Dr. Brian Joseph McNamara? He was an honorable man who lived a full life in the fifty-four years on Earth that he was granted. It was important for me to honor my brother on behalf of all of his siblings.

Brian's Funeral, St. Bernadette Catholic Church, Westlake, Ohio – April 28, 1998
Excerpts from the Eulogy by Shelly McNamara

As many of you know, Brian was the eldest of fifteen children. He was down-to-earth, easy-going, and extremely unpretentious!

For Brian, the term "doctor" was an open door to care for and help people. It was not a title to open doors in social circles. He never took himself that seriously.

Everyone at the hospital called him "Mac"—no need for fancy titles or ceremony.

For many of us, he was a role model. He was a father figure who filled an empty void.

He triggered the deepest laughter and the brightest smile from his greatest admirer, our mother.

Brian always said that "I was Mommy's baby." But I knew the truth.

Brian Joseph McNamara

A restless soul
Always seemed to have somewhere to go or something to do
A restless soul now quieted, safe, and at home with his maker

Our hearts are heavy
Our hearts are sad

But lightened by knowing that when our Mother passes on—soon
She will be met at the Gates of Heaven by her first-born son
Brian, always with a special place in Mom's heart
Now there to greet her and bring her home

Brian Joseph McNamara, dear brother
Forget what we didn't say or didn't do in this lifetime together
There's always a special place in our heart for you

Rest in peace, dear brother. We love you very much.

Shelly

I can't help but wonder if we weren't both unknowingly "blinded" for some portion of our time together on earth. I have learned that judgment goes both ways—and that the moments we spent in judgment or walking past one another were a shared responsibility. Maybe, it was more my fear of judgment than judgment that really existed. I will never know what we missed with one another, but I do know that we had love and mutual respect. No regrets. I also know that it brought me some peace and closure to honor him, to release him, and to remind myself to leave behind judgment and to avoid regret. Regret is a difficult emotion to carry around for a lifetime.

I Regret

If I were to wish
For anything

If I were to
Regret anything

I wish that I had
Loved more and
Judged less

I just didn't see it
Didn't see you

I regret

We all have the chance to begin again, but it requires us to discover our regrets, our wrongs, and then to have the courage to make different choices.

What regrets or wrongs do you carry?

What can you do to release those regrets? Is it time to make new choices? It's never too late to begin again.

Is there something you can do to reframe a situation or a relationship to free yourself or the other person?

5. The Day Will Come

The day will come, the moment will pass, when you will be called as different in a way that says less, or less than . . .

It was Mother's Day 2013, early evening, when I learned about it. Our daughter had been bullied by a girl who had once been a friend.

The conversation started like this: "Can I talk to you both? I want you to know how much I love you. I can't imagine having or wanting any other parents. You have given me so much—so much love. The most important thing you have taught me is to love and accept everyone. I try to do that. I need to share something with you. I don't want to hurt you. I just need to tell you something. Alexis has been bullying me. Her favorite thing to do is to walk up to a group of girls and say, 'Hey, did you know that . . .' She then proceeds to talk badly about our family.

"She demeans you because you are gay. She demeans me because I have two moms. I don't want you to feel bad . . . I just need you to know."

I recall the sentiment—the feelings of sadness, confusion, and pain, the kind of deep pain felt when your child is under siege. It is a unique pain. Yet, our daughter's words eased that pain: "You two are a model of kindness. You have given us love and showed us what real love looks and feels like. I know how lucky my sisters and I are. I will get through this. I have you and our family."

My heart sank—tears streamed down my face. It's not that I never thought our child would be bullied. In fact, our child has the profile that bullies look for. She's kind. She's quiet. She's thoughtful, and she is very sensitive. Frankly, it's not just the "gay parent thing" that made her the target. I know that now—now that we are a few years past this conversation. The three of us cried that evening and talked at length. I did go to bed that night feeling a bit angry with Alexis. But, more than that, I felt sorry for her. I had enough insight to know that her bullying came from "the lack of" in her own life. Our daughter is not and will not be her only target. Bullies feed off of vulnerability.

As we sat together processing this conversation, Cindy and I marveled at the strength and wisdom of our daughter. To be the target of hate. To rise above that hate and worry most about hurting her parents. A strong, wise, and thoughtful child. We had done something right, and we both hated seeing the pain in her eyes. It was the wisdom and love that poured out from her heart that got us all through that evening and the ensuing days of conversation.

Bullying isn't unique to our daughter's experience. The data shows that about 20 percent of students ages twelve to eighteen nationwide experience bullying.[4] Bullying is unwanted, aggressive behavior toward another person or group. The most frequently targeted children tend to be those who are perceived as different than their peers, such as LGBTQ+ and youth with disabilities.[5] My learning and life experience tell me that children who have built a level of self-esteem and confidence in self are less likely to bully. Children raised in homes by parents who don't label those who are different as "less than" are also less likely to bully. Children model what they see and experience around them.

---

4 StopBullying.gov: https://www.stopbullying.gov/resources/facts#stats

5 CDC: https://www.cdc.gov/mmwr/volumes/67/ss/pdfs/ss6708a1-h.pdf

The costs of bullying are high. Children who have been bullied have greater levels of anxiety, depression, and more difficulty with school. Adults also bully and are bullied. I have witnessed bullying in my professional work. The same principle applies—the better we feel about ourselves, the less likely we are to bully. The work of getting and being comfortable with our authentic selves is critical and important for us and everyone around us. People in pain can cause deep pain in others.

What this bully underestimated was the power of love. Our daughter not only survived, but in the end, thrived, because she gained the wisdom and deep insight that are often only born out of deep pain. She built empathy, maturity, and depth of character. She had enough confidence in herself and her parents that she rose above.

I will never, ever forget that moment.

I anticipated these situations, and many years earlier, had written . . .

You Have Been Chosen

The day will come
The moment will pass
When you will be called as different
In a way that says "Less"
Less than

We will be waiting
To step in
To give you the love
To remind you of the reason

That God made you special
Gave you two moms

He called you to teach
Love One Another
Not One
But All

You are the chosen teachers
We are the committed parents
Always there
To remind you

Why you have been chosen to lead

I chose to be a mom. Cindy and I chose to be parents—together. Our girls have full lives. They have great friends, real friends—the kind who lift them up, visit when they are sick, and defend them when others call them "less than." Most importantly, every day, they know that for me and Cindy, they are always "more than." And in those few moments that fear and hatred have stared them in the eyes . . . we have their backs. We rise above together. Our life journey has taught us to value our time together; we have lost family members unexpectedly, and we know the pain of being treated as less than. We value our love.

Next Time

Next time—you might regret
The times you walked past me
The times you looked away

Next time—I might not be here
To hear your sorrows
To forgive your regrets
To heal your wounds

Next time—you might really miss me
Because I may be gone

We might not have a next time

I have often reflected on those moments of judgment or pain inflicted on me or us. It hurts to be minimized or treated as less than. After one of those moments, it occurred to me that the pain may actually be reversed one day. I realized that those who judge or reject may one day live with the pain of regret. Regret is that feeling which settles in when you realize that you won't ever know "what could have been" because there will not be a next time. Life changed. Time moved on. There is no next time.

Have you treated someone as "less than?" Or, have you been treated as "less than?" Where is there room to build a bridge to a better relationship?

Is there someone in your life waiting nearby to heal your sorrows, forgive your regrets, or heal your wounds? How can you connect?

Where can you create a "next time?"

6. Level Set

We are taught to see things and people as better than and less than; why not "different than?"

Procter & Gamble World Headquarters, Cincinnati, Ohio – March 2012

It is truly my privilege and honor to introduce today's speaker, Shelly McNamara. Shelly is a great colleague, a trusted friend and partner, and a remarkable human being.

I'm a passionate advocate of the power of story. Stories are a powerful way to bring to life big ideas, purpose, brands . . . and people. They make us who we are and they help to articulate what makes each of us unique. Stories are how we SHARE a part of ourselves with others, to bring people together and enrich our collective experiences. When we hear, understand, and respect each other's stories, we take an important step forward in unleashing our full potential.

The story you'll hear from Shelly today is genuine, poignant, authentic, and focused on creating a better P&G and a better community. A community where stories from every person—gay or straight—are shared, understood, embraced, and valued. A community where LGBT people are always treated as respected equals. A community where LGBT people are never, ever thought of as "less than" . . . which, unfortunately, happens way too often.

If any of us cannot be ourselves, the company loses a part of the richness of who we are as individual contributors, and that means we are not doing all we can to serve consumers. The community we want to build at P&G is one where we genuinely care for each other and where we ALL work together at our full capacity to win. We want a community of human beings that rely on each other, where everyone brings their "whole selves" to work, in order to serve every human being on the planet.

So, I ask you to think about this as you hear Shelly's powerful stories and words of wisdom. Take her calls to action to heart. And I encourage you to share your story, connect with others, and bring your whole self to work to build the community we want at P&G.

Marc Pritchard,
P&G Chief Brand Officer

A moment of honor. A moment of responsibility. It was March 7, 2012, when I stood on the stage at the Procter & Gamble world headquarters in Cincinnati, Ohio, to share my story publicly for the first time (much of which I've captured in this book). We were live-streaming to multiple locations around the world. This was the moment to give voice to those who had been silenced and alleviate fear for those who see us (in the LGBTQ+ community) as people to be feared, judged, and maybe even despised. I walked onstage, stepping into the next phase of my life's work, and launched the next wave of equality and inclusion for the lesbian, gay, bisexual, and transgender employees at P&G, as well as for anyone who had ever been made to feel less than. The words came out . . .

I am Shelly McNamara, the Vice President of HR in Beauty & Grooming. I am a mother, a life partner, a sister, and an aunt.

I am also gay.

I don't claim or try to represent all LGBT people or all same sex parents. I have my own story, just as each of you do.

A few troubling statistics:

Most LGBT people worry about being out at work—54% of us.

Only 39% of us feel comfortable introducing our spouse or partner to a colleague or boss.

Most, if not all, of us have experienced a level of rejection or judgment that left us with emotional wounds that can last a lifetime.

Every day, somewhere in our country, there is a teenager or young adult who seriously questions whether life is worth living.

Why should I care? Why should P&G care?

When LGBT people take energy to hide who they are or how they live life, we waste time, energy, and capability. We miss relationships. We miss connections. We miss creating something together. It all translates to loss. There is tremendous loss for us as human beings. There is tremendous loss for P&G as a company. There is tremendous loss for those around us. It's quite simple—when people hold back who they are, it's a loss for of all of us.

Why do we choose to hide? We live in a world that tells us we are "less than." We aren't due the same privileges or respect as straight people, and somehow, we just need to settle for what we get, even if it is less than. I decided a long time ago that this wasn't okay with me . . . that I was going to live a full life, no matter how uncomfortable it made some people around me feel. I wish the same for everyone. Even for those who don't understand or accept us for who we are.

I have hopes and wishes for all of us in the room today; for those who identify as lesbian, gay, bisexual or transgender, I wish for you to . . .

Live authentically. Live true to who you are. Don't hide and don't apologize.

Make choices consistent with who you are and what you want out of life. Don't give away your power to choose. Don't give away your power, period.

Not accept "less than"—expect and demand the same privileges as the people who are straight. No blanks. No pauses.

To our straight friends and allies, I wish you will . . .

Learn more about who we are and our unique struggles.

Share your privileges—proactively break barriers on our behalf.

I also ask that you not . . .

Call being gay a choice. It's who I am. One aspect of my identity.

Call it my lifestyle. It's my family.

Call my family alternative—that sounds like the choice no one wants.

Treat us as "less than."

I have chosen to live a full life, a happy life. I live authentically. Despite many obstacles and much judgment, I made the choices that have shaped my life. I chose my career, my friends, and how I spend my time. And I chose my partner (okay, so she might tell you that she chose me). Together, we chose how we will raise our children.

I live authentically. I encourage you to do the same. I don't accept less than. I don't expect any of you to either. Being gay isn't who I am, but it is a part of who I am. It's an important part of who I am, because it's the gateway to understanding me and my family. I am unique and we are a unique family.

Our decision to have children was an easy one for me. I saw myself as a mother long before I saw myself as an HR manager, partner, sister, or any other role I play in life. It made some people uncomfortable and frankly, in my earlier days at P&G, I couldn't see myself working here and being a lesbian mother. I saw too many around me who seemed very narrow in their definitions of life, love, and privilege.

It worked because I met and worked with straight colleagues who were willing to share their privilege and proactively support me. This support came in many ways—mentors who coached me on who to work with and for, and whom to avoid. Colleagues who connected with me in authentic ways.

I developed the skills and gained the experiences I needed for the career I aspired to have. I sought out LGBT supportive managers. I observed. I listened to people I trusted. I networked. I shared some of my personal struggles, some of our struggles, with leaders I trusted and those I wanted to influence or change for the better. I asked for their support. I asked their advice on which leaders I needed to avoid—those blinded by prejudice and homophobia. I built a network that included some with political and organizational power, some with deep human insight, and some who offered me the shoulder to cry on when I hit those big bumps in the road. I knew what I needed, and I built a system that provided that.

Open doors for your LGBT colleagues. Connect with them. Help them connect with others so that they get the career and personal support they need and deserve. Ask yourself the tough questions.

I am blessed with many straight allies and friends at P&G who never make me or my family feel different or less—thank you!

It's great to have people in my life who know that . . .

Love Makes A Family

What if I told you that
Love makes a family
That God places children
With parents he chooses

That your view of love
Doesn't match mine

That I have a love for my children
That drowns out your judgment
Your exclusion of me as a parent worthy to serve

I answered my call
What about you?

Our children have given us so many gifts.

The gifts of love and freedom have been profound. It was the arrival of our three girls that gave me the peace and conviction to be comfortable as a gay person. I realized that only by loving myself and living from a place of peace could I truly love my children and give them the sense of peace and belonging in the world that they so deserved—that each of us deserves.

I know that our struggle for acceptance and freedom is not over yet. Every day, there are gay or lesbian people struggling for acceptance from their family or work colleagues. These people don't work "somewhere else"— they work at P&G. I know, because some of them reach out to me and others for support. Every day, there is a gay teenager somewhere in this country asking themselves if life is worth living in the face of the overt prejudice and bullying that they experience.

I carry with me a *Cincinnati Enquirer* from a few months back; on the front page, a politician proudly states their desire to maintain laws that discriminate against LGBT people. On the inside cover, the obituary for an eighteen-year-old young man who committed suicide. He gave up trying to live in a world that made him feel less than. I keep this because it's a constant reminder that I need to be a voice for those who can't speak or aren't given the platform like the one I have been given here today.

I do know there are many good things and many good people (like the straight allies in the room who chose to be here with us today). Yes, there is always hope and inspiration around us if we are open enough to see it and receive it.

The struggle is ours. Not mine or yours. I want inclusion of all, without exception. My freedoms do not in any way detract from yours. In fact, victory is when we all feel free to live and be our whole selves.

We should all feel free.

As I look back on this speech, I am especially struck by how simplistic, in a sense, these wishes are. These are things that should be unconditionally available and granted to all, yet they are not.

Too many people live from a place of fear and ignorance. We inherit labels and lies that tell us that anyone different from us is somehow "less than." We inherit biases from the world around us. Those biases create a distance that keeps us apart.

What is bias? Bias is a particular tendency, trend, inclination, feeling or opinion—especially one that is preconceived or unreasoned. Biases often lead us to believe that some people are better than others. These conscious and unconscious biases cause us to be drawn to people with similar backgrounds, cultures, religions, families, and life experiences to us. If we keep our interactions and relationships here, we stunt our growth as human beings.

As human beings, we all have biases and prejudice. We do, however, get to choose whether or not we remain hostage to these or free ourselves through choice—the choice to experience a broader range and diversity of humanity. Our biases don't ever go away, but we can build self-awareness that enables us to "intervene in the automatic" when those biases take over our mind and actions. Personal growth is a choice.

What is prejudice? It's a preconceived opinion that is not based on reason or actual experience. Like files stored in our brains, we have opinions stored about people and things that are not based on anything sound or experienced. We come to believe things about "them" and "those." Most often, the harshest critique is thrust at those whom we know the least or not at all.

The key influencers of opinion have enormous responsibility. What they say and how they say it drives perception and opinion. This group includes parents, religious institutions, advertisers, media, and visible leaders. They have formed a powerful narrative in our heads that establishes bias and prejudice as a replacement for individual experiences. Too often, they have used their platforms to fuel falsehoods and fears surrounding specific groups of people. This fear and hatred are both unfounded and unwarranted and prompt people to behave and act in ways that are destructive.

The brain has developed a bio-evolutionary adaptation of "short cutting"—in this sense, it often uses stereotypes and broad identification as ways to quickly process data and stimuli to determine actions needed or called for by the situation. This is an important capability, particularly in threatening situations. That being said, we must acknowledge how this process can foster judgment and preconceptions.

I am not immune to bias and prejudice. Like every human being on the planet, I have both. The work I need to do is to build my own self-awareness, to notice when my vision is being blurred by filters of bias and prejudice that prevent me from listening and learning, from seeing and experiencing each human being as a unique person. I'm certain that my own assumptions and biases have kept me distant from some. I also know that my experience interacting with so many different people around the world has taught me to give every person I meet the space to be their unique self—without judgment.

I do believe that when bias and prejudice go unchecked and unchallenged, we create a level of fear and judgment, a line of pain that we need to erase.

They Crossed the Line

They crossed the line
One by one
"If you have ever been made fun of for being . . .
Black—Overweight—Jewish—or Gay

Cross the line

If you have ever been called a 'sissy' or soft for
Crying—showing your feelings
Or showing you care

Cross the line

Cross the line of pain

The line we all created
The place we taught our children to go
And send others

To dump their feelings of fear and self-doubt

We created the world and line of bigotry
How can we erase it?

This poem was inspired by a deeply impactful exercise that I participated in during many diversity training sessions. The facilitator read each statement aloud, pausing after to allow those who identified with it to step forward.

We all stood on the same line at the start, but the "questions of pain" separated those who had been targeted from those who had been protected. I have now participated in this exercise multiple times, and each time, there is a clear pattern that emerges: the deep pain is not evenly distributed. There is always a group that has been mostly spared, and those that carry heavier burdens. I felt my own personal pain deeply—the labels and bias that had been thrown my way over the years. I felt the pain of others, in and outside of the room, who I know suffered greatly. I could see and feel the circle and cycle of pain we have all created, perpetuated, or enabled through our silence. I decided in that moment that it was time for that pain to end. I don't want my children, or yours, to "cross the line" ever again.

We need to start by noticing privileges granted or not. I have often found it is those of us *with* privilege who don't even see the privileges we have until they are taken away or threatened. Some live with that feeling every day.

I don't share this as an indictment; I offer it as an invitation to those who are less often targeted to expand your lenses and learn about the experiences and the pain suffered by those who have "crossed the line" much more often than you. Internalized shame and pain destroy individual human beings and those around them. What if we could all help prevent and eliminate this pain?

What I know is that when children are told that who they are isn't good enough, they learn self-doubt and self-hatred. When children learn that "those people" are to be feared or judged, we create distance and divisions that destroy. We make it nearly impossible for them to learn from others who are different—they don't have a strong foundation to stand on.

What can we do? I believe we need to start by . . . encouraging authenticity.

"Authentic," as in genuine, original, and trustworthy.

Living authentically didn't come easily for me. As the youngest of fifteen children raised by a single mother, I lived a modest life, but one filled with love. I pursued academic excellence to gain independence, affirmation, and unconditional support. I was never perfect, but I pursued perfection relentlessly. Being gay wasn't a part of my plan. It didn't fit with my image of perfection, or my desire to be "the good girl." The images I saw and the judgment I heard from friends, family, and religion told me that being gay was "less than," that I was "less than." I struggled for years to reconcile who I was with the expectations around me.

Eventually, I came to terms with that aspect of my identity: I was a lesbian. The "eventually" finally arrived because I met and fell in love with my soulmate.

I met Cindy in the fall of 1981 at the University of Michigan in Ann Arbor, Michigan. We were instant friends. Cindy is reserved, contemplative, and deeply private (a true New Englander). I am talkative, quite open, and not known to be shy. Yet, on a foundational level, we share some important character traits and values: honesty, integrity, kindness, and a priority for family and friends. We developed a deep friendship that evolved into a deep love by the spring of 1983. I fell in love with Cindy's kind and loving heart. There is no one more kind or loving on the planet. No one. She has helped me discover my full humanity and full self more than any other.

That being said, the journey to peace was not an easy one. The world around me judged and disdained those that were LGBTQ+.

I remember one of the first people who rejected me for being my true self; she was a close childhood friend. A person I trusted with my dreams, hopes, and fears growing up. She stopped talking to me—abandoned our friendship—when she discovered I was gay. The childhood friend I'd felt the most connected to had distanced herself from me. One of my worst fears seemed to come true.

Fifteen years post high school graduation, her father passed away. He was an Irish man who was very proud of his heritage, a kind and giving man who'd always reached out to me when I visited their home. I was unable to make his funeral service, so I sent green carnations to honor our shared Irish heritage.

My friend called me a week later to thank me for the flowers and to apologize for the distance, for the silence I had experienced for so many years. It was a church sermon on homophobia that sparked the phone call: a minister called out the injustices committed by those who use God as a way to minimize, punish, and exclude lesbian and gay people.

I wish the hurt had instantly disappeared when she apologized, but it didn't. Some wounds, like those that attack the very core of your identity, can last a lifetime. Or maybe the wounds heal, but the shame leaves an indelible mark.

The Day I Lost A Friend

The day I lost a friend . . .
I was smiling, bright and happy
I was caring and concerned for others
I was myself

And then I lost my friend
She liked me for my laughter, insights and caring ways
But her smile soon faded
And so too did her friendship

All that I had said
All that I had done
All that I was to her
Lost . . . in a moment's time

All because of who I am
And because of that, I lost my friend

That hurt rested deep within my soul and my psyche. I maintained my love and care for my dear friend, but I was deeply wounded.

For a period of my life, I learned how to be kind and friendly without making friends. If I didn't make any new friends, I wouldn't have any to lose. It was a (subconscious) logic I came to accept.

I had internalized the homophobia that surrounded me. This self-doubt and shame drove me to create distance with others. Or maybe, just maybe, I avoided building friendships to escape what I most disdained—being judged for simply being who I am, the true source of shame.

This pattern of engaging (or rather, not engaging) lasted for many years. A few did make it through the wall I'd built, but I missed many opportunities for authentic connections. A coworker, Heather, is one example of that loss; it was my last conversation with her that triggered me to admit the painful truth that I kept people at a distance to protect myself from hurt and judgment.

At the time, Heather and I had worked closely together for two or three years, yet our conversations never made it past the surface level. In fact, I waited until a week before she was moving out of the state to tell her about my life, my identity, and my life partner. She was deeply saddened by the loss of the friendship that never really evolved because I kept a distance.

As Heather mourned the human connection I'd chosen to avoid, I reflected and thought, *maybe judgment goes both ways?* My "pre-judgment" of so many others had left me without for fear of being judged. We fear what we don't understand. We fear those about whom we have been told lies. We fear the hurt of rejection when we are in the group that is often misrepresented and misunderstood. Sometimes it feels safer to remain a mystery and unknown than to risk judgment and loss. Judgment does go both ways, and we all lose out.

I still fight my tendency to create distance as a mechanism to protect myself. Many of us choose social distance over the risk, the potential for judgment, and the ensuing hurt. There were many "Heathers" along my path; she was just the first one to call me out on the choice I'd made to keep a distance—to stay disconnected and safe.

Can You Let Me in Now?

Time passes
Life passes
Why focus on things that bring distance between us?

I pass by you daily
Do I see, acknowledge, and celebrate you?

Do I judge what you are, who you see, and how you look?

Our lives have kept us apart
My judgment has kept us apart

I am older and wiser now
I see you so rarely
I wish to see you more

I long to share a moment with you
If only to share a smile or word of advice
Or maybe a tear for all of the time and
Pain that has passed

I once passed you by with only a frown and a scorn
As I judged what you were
Who you saw and
How you looked

If only I had known what is so clear to me now
All of those years since past

Can you let me in now?

I am in the process of unlearning habits that were designed to protect me from judgment and pain. I perfected these habits over many years. Today, as I write, I see how my choices, my fears, and my judgment kept me disconnected from others.

I needed to heal, to walk through the pain of judgment thrust upon me by people I trusted and loved. It's this healing that showed me judgment goes both ways. I needed to reflect on my own judgment, fears, and biases. It's the healing work I did that allowed me to grow.

Today, I have deep and lasting friendships with a diverse mix of people. I am grateful to my friends that know and show that "love is love," which means that love comes in many forms. My friends from countries outside of the US have taught me the universality of humanity—that no matter where you are in the world, the basic human needs for safety, love, growth, and community are shared and matter most.

I wonder, *what if I choose to accept you for who you are, and what you are? What would I need to unlearn?* With critical reflection, I can acknowledge how some foundational components of my life may have fostered judgment. Religion taught me to minimize and label some and elevate others. Family taught me to love parts of me and to hide and hate other parts. Society taught me to seek beauty, brains, and conformity, even if it left the real "me" behind.

When do we take off our masks? What do we lose waiting to find the right day, right time? What happens if we give ourselves permission to love? To hear? To forgive? To be who we are meant to be? No masks. No pretense. No labels. *Authentic.*

I think back to March of 2012, and what it took for me to get on that stage and share my story. That moment triggered work with deep meaning and purpose. It's been quite a journey.

In the past eight years, I have traveled to every region of the world to share the following message: it's time to "level set." I aspire to see each person as different, but equally magnificent. My motivation is simple: I believe that we are stronger and better together. I know that great communities, companies, and neighborhoods begin with love and acceptance for all. No exceptions.

Level Set

We are taught to see things and people
As better than and less than

Why not "different than?"

We have this need to level up and down
I win—you lose
You win—I lose
One up—one down
Always

Why not "level set?"
Grant you space to be you
And I get to be me

We no longer need
To make one better than
To make one "less than"

What will it take to "level set?"
To see each other as different
But equally magnificent

Create space where everyone can shine

I am fortunate to work for a company that is committed to creating a world free from gender, racial, and sexual orientation bias . . . bias of all kinds. I have led transformations in our talent systems and culture to ensure that we build an outstanding and diverse pipeline of talent for Procter & Gamble that reflects the diverse population of consumers around the world. I am proud of my company and my colleagues for taking on this work. We care deeply about improving the lives of people throughout our world.

A few hours after I delivered my speech on March 7, 2012, an employee stopped by my office to say to me, "You will never know who this was, but today you saved a life. I want you to hear and know that. Today you saved a life." I left that conversation believing that there was a human being contemplating the choice to live or die. My story—my life story and life lessons triggered a choice to pick life over death. I knew then that authentic storytelling was a core part of my life's work.

⸻

Who do you see as "less than?"

What are you willing to unlearn or leave behind?

What will you do to "level set?"

7. The Power of Choice

When I make choices that are consistent with who I am, what I bring, why I'm here, I live more fully—I live more freely . . .

I had a deep belief that Cindy and I were meant to be parents, that this privilege and responsibility was part of our path. I know this choice was the right choice. A glimpse into our home reveals three amazing young women who love and live with passion and are proud of the family they have. They will make a mark on the world. They have been loved and supported for who they are. They have much of their lives yet to define and live. But what I do know, as a mother to these three girls, is that their joy and big hearts will make the world a better place. It is my greatest honor to be one of their moms.

I vividly remember the moment, so many years ago, when I chose, we chose, authenticity over shame. In fact, we intentionally and thoughtfully made two critical choices that would shape our lives and the lives of our children:

We would not hide in shame or feel shame because of biases and beliefs that others held and often projected on us.

We would be and live as our authentic selves. No pretending. Our children deserved to have parents who showed up fully.

We made these choices, but we still work at this every day. Resisting shame and choosing authenticity were critical choices for us, healthy choices.

Our choices manifested in a critical and private conversation. It was July 1997, and I was sitting across from my new manager, Scott. I was nervous. After a long pause, I finally spoke: "I have some great news to share . . . and I need your help. I'm going to be a mother in a few months. My partner, Cindy, is pregnant with our child. I don't know how people in our business will react or behave toward me when they learn that I'm gay and expecting a child."

Without hesitation, Scott said, "Congratulations. There is no greater honor or joy than being a parent. And, if anyone here gives you any problems, I will take care of it. You have my full support. If somebody gives you a problem or treats you badly, send them to me, and I'll take care of it."

I was instantly out of the corporate closet. I was relieved and afraid. I felt free. Most of all, I felt proud. Cindy and I had made the choice to live free and open. I did not want shame to become a part of my character or my feelings about self. I chose, and we chose, to be authentic and to live authentically. Our children would not learn shame from us. The world would not always be kind or validating, but we would have love and each other. We would replace shame with authenticity.

I really didn't completely come out in all facets of my life until I was weeks away from being a mom. This was a bold choice in 1997. At the time, most lesbian, gay, bisexual, and transgender people were not open. It's hard to know just how many people openly identified as LGBTQ+ back then, in part because the US government only started tracking LGBTQ+ identification in the 2016 census. There was a strong anti-LGBTQ+ sentiment throughout the '90s, particularly in politics. For perspective, Ellen DeGeneres lost her show in 1997 after she came out as a lesbian. It was a precarious and difficult time for an LGBTQ+ person. *New York Times* journalist Frank Rich labeled a "homophobic epidemic of '98," which spiked with the murder of a twenty-one-year-old gay University of Wyoming student, Matthew Shepard.[6] It was a scary time.

Choice has been an important word in my life. There was an important choice that we made, which was the choice to not have our children learn shame. I had been shamed by different people for being a lesbian. I had been shamed for being different, and I never wanted our children to learn shame from us.

I knew people would try to shame them. Human beings have a way of doing that. Our life journeys bring us shame in different ways, but if we can prevent it, or at least if we actively choose to keep shame away, that will be a good start. There were those who shamed us to our face, and some who chose to when we weren't in the room. The shaming came in different forms, but always with words of harsh judgment.

We went on to have two more daughters. In early 2000, we had twins. Carrying twins with my 5'1" body frame was challenging. I spent my first trimester with ten straight weeks of nausea, and I was on bed rest for the final six weeks of the pregnancy. In my final weeks, when I was out in public (for doctors' appointments), people would turn and stare at me as if I were a paranormal creature.

I carried Kate and Nicole just two days short of thirty-eight weeks, which translates to full term for a twin pregnancy. Delivering them took three trips to the hospital, two inductions, and a C-section, but they finally arrived. These two girls were born exactly the same weight, 7 lbs., 2.8 oz.—a lot of baby for this small frame to carry!

Kate was "Baby A," which means she was first in line to come out—our first indication of her strength and innate leadership. Nicole had flipped at twenty-eight weeks to move into a head-down, delivery-

---

6 *The Atlantic*: https://www.theatlantic.com/politics/archive/2013/04/how-america-got-past-the-anti-gay-politics-of-the-90s/266976/

suitable position. This was shocking to my doctor, and something she refused to believe until the ultrasound confirmed the flip. This was an appropriate move, and foreshadowed Nicole the gymnast.

Our full journey into parenting had begun. I felt a sense of peace and freedom. The arrival of our daughters was an essential part of our life path. I knew that I loved these three girls long before they arrived in our arms. They truly gave me a sense of peace, calm, and purpose that I had never before felt, never before known. I wrote this poem in their honor . . .

The Gift of Freedom

Among so many other things, little peanut
You've given me freedom
Given us freedom

It's an inner strength, an inner peace
I've never before felt
I've never before known

It's an outer voice to claim what's mine
To take what's mine
To take what's ours

It's the space to make our family
The voice to name our love
The calm to live amidst the storm
That inevitably awaits us
As those around us miss the message of God
Miss the message of love

We live our lives more fully—more connected
We share our love more openly—more freely
It's you that grant us this gift
The gift to know, love, and publicly be oneself
The true gift of freedom

Our role as parents has been validated over the years. Friends, teachers, and family members have extended love, so much love. Sometimes the validation and support came from unexpected places.

In June 2004, at Ali's kindergarten graduation, Mrs. G approached us: "I want to tell you how much I loved having Ali in my class. She is smart, respectful, and gives generously to my special needs kids. She is such a thoughtful, sensitive child. I know this doesn't happen by chance. She is who she is because of the two of you. You have done a wonderful job as parents."

My ears rang with the words once spoken to me: ". . . you will ruin the lives of the children." In that moment, as I listened to those kind words about Ali, some of the pain, some of those deep feelings of "less than" that had previously stained my heart slowly melted away.

There are people like Mrs. G. She saw two parents standing in front of her. She acknowledged a wonderful child. She knew the significance for the lesbian parents to be acknowledged and celebrated. I know there are people who judge me, judge us, as less than and believe we are not worthy of parenting. Parenting is a selfless job, if done right. I knew that not everyone had the wisdom and grace of Mrs. G, and I had written about my fears years earlier.

A Letter for My Daughters

There will be those who will not like you
They will scorn, frown, and resent
Your very existence

They will pass you by, mock, tease, and never invite you
To their birthday parties

They think that gay parents are less than
With nothing of value to teach

Their eyes are blinded by prejudice, fear, and hatred
Things you never learned from us

We've taught you kindness—share it abundantly
We've given you love, lots of love
Draw from it to keep you whole

We've given you faith, trust, and confidence in God, Self, and Others
You will need them often
Remember, your two moms came together
To create a family and legacy of love
You are an integral part of that plan

Yes, there are those who don't see us in this light
Be patient and show them that love has no boundaries

I was fortunate to work with colleagues who believed and behaved as if everyone was valued and included. They proactively supported me and often used their status and voices to help drive important cultural and policy shifts that created a more even playing field. They knew that being heterosexual in our society comes with a "higher status" that is granted greater privileges. They were committed to expanding and sharing the privileges equally that they took for granted.

The concept of privilege is an important one. Privilege is about having inherent rights or advantages. At the root of privilege sits expanded choices and benefits. For those of us in the LGBTQ+ community, being human hasn't been enough for us to have the same rights. We have and continue to work for equality in housing, employment, and health care. I am fortunate to have friends and colleagues who have consistently fought for me to have the same range of choices and benefits that they had.

This support for me and others in my community showed up in the daily "small things," like using the term "partner" and not immediately assuming that I or anyone else was heterosexual. It showed up in the bigger things—the support for marriage equality. They, too, celebrated when Cindy and I were able to marry after thirty years together. And, there were the important policy changes they supported in areas like health care benefits that enabled all three of our daughters to be on my insurance.

The choice to be parents was a big choice, an important choice. Upon sharing the news that we were going to be parents, a family member told us that we were selfish for having children, that children of gay parents would struggle and suffer. We stepped outside the range of "acceptable privilege." We were accepted as a couple, but gay parents crossed the line for some, who deemed the privilege of parenting outside of our reach.

Peering in from Without

I look from within at the world
In which I find myself
In which we find ourselves

I see faces that choose only to recognize parts of me privately
Parts of me publicly
"This is my son, Jack, his wife, Jill and their darling son, Michael
Uhhh, yeah, and this is my sister, Shelly . . .
And this is Cindy."

The validation—the invalidation
The love they choose to ignore
The pain they never see
Relationships validated
Relationships invalidated

The love they publicly ignore
I privately keep for my own
To nurture, to keep me safe
From a world that forces me to
Peer in from without

We make choices every day, both by what we do and what we don't do. Whom we talk to and whom we talk about. What we talk about and what we choose not to talk about. When I selected the theme "choose love" for my writing, I realized that it actually is a choice, and a powerful one. The most common opposite choices, I believe, are fear and hate. The choice to love gives me a sense of peace and calm like no other choice I have made. I choose love.

What this choice requires me to do is to not judge. There's a big difference between being discerning and being judgmental or judging. Discernment is the ability to judge well. To be perceptive, wise, and discriminating in our choices. We learn to be discerning and make good choices through education and life experience. For example, I am discerning about where I walk alone at night. Discernment is a helpful life guide and compass. Judgment is often rooted in a belief that one person is inherently better than another.

When it comes to people, I ask myself, *why do I have to judge?* I wonder if it isn't fear that keeps people in a place of judgment. Maybe we are too often socialized to fear anyone who is different. What good comes out of judging who they are, what they do, who they love, and how they dress? Nothing good comes out of it.

Making Choices

When I make choices that are consistent with
Who I am
What I bring
Why I'm here

I live more fully
I live more freely

I am able to accept your choices
Who you are
What you bring
Why you're here

Being more fully me
Allows you to be more fully you
We not only co-exist
We co-create

To me, choosing love is about being fully present and open to anyone and everyone I encounter. It's really freeing. I live authentically. I encourage everyone around me to do the same. I don't accept less than. I don't expect anyone else to either. Being gay isn't who I am, but it is one aspect of my identity. We are all multifaceted, multi-dimensional beings.

We have raised our daughters to live authentically. To be proud of their family and the life and love they have been given. They have challenging moments, like we all do. The fact that they have gay parents has brought them some unique and deep life lessons, but I believe, at my core, that the enduring lesson for them is that love has no boundaries.

What or whom do you judge—perhaps out of fear?

Are you living your most authentic life?

What choices have you made? And what new choices do you need or want to make?

How are you encouraging your family members to be their most authentic selves?

8. Privileges Granted—or Not

Some clubs come with rights and privileges. Others are marked by their absence.

Throughout my life, I have searched for meaning and purpose. I recall sitting next to my mother in church at the age of seven or eight, when it suddenly occurred to me that I didn't know "where I was" ten years earlier. The concept of life beyond was a difficult concept, and it frightened me to consider that I may have been somewhere other than with my mother. I edged closer to her. I was unsettled emotionally and intellectually.

That left me wondering, *why are we here on this earth?* My religious and spiritual curiosity over the years guided my energy toward learning and growth. I deeply desired to evolve both my soul and my being to be a better, more loving human. My poetry and storytelling became physical manifestations of my lifelong search for meaning and purpose.

As the years progressed, I came to see both the value and significance of a life that often put me "on the edges." Being different from the norm gave me a unique perspective, built empathy, and deepened my understanding of our journey as human beings. And so, I wrote . . .

On the Edges

They think there's one straight line
That takes you down the middle
Of the road

What about the beauty, the excitement
That lies along the edges?

The center line—the straight line
Takes you to the places
You have already been

I invite you to explore the edges
To go outside the lines
To find the beauty
Not on the straight line
To find the beauty that comes
From exploring and living on the edges

This is where I have found the insight
On the edges
Not down the middle of the road

When you live on the edges as members of communities that are granted less status or privilege, you have unique experiences and moments.

One such moment happened on December 17, 2004, the day Cindy and I became legal parents of our own children. On this day, I officially gave up my legal rights to Kate and Nicole so that Cindy and I could adopt them at the bottom of the same legal document. On document #2, Cindy (as Ali's birth mother) officially gave up her rights to Ali so that we could both legally adopt Ali at the bottom of the same page. At that time, this was the only way we could both become legal parents of our own children. In fact, until 2015, the state of Ohio did not allow two people of the same gender to be parents of a child. I actually resigned from P&G and returned to the company eighteen months later so we could move to a state where we could legally become parents of our own children.

December 17, 2004 was a special day at the courthouse in New York: Adoption Day. The halls were lined with children of all ages, races, and socio-economic backgrounds. It was a beautiful rainbow of humanity. Many of these children were being adopted by their foster parents. What a joy to see. Our girls were being adopted by their own parents—the two people who had loved and cared for them since the day they were born. We'd anxiously awaited the arrival of that day.

We entered the judge's courtroom, where he warmly welcomed our girls by asking each of them to pick out a stuffed animal from the assortment that lay in front of them. Ali selected a brown bear, Kate went for the brown dog, and Nicole scooped up the yellow duck. They each brought their new friend to the judge's table, where a stack of papers awaiting our signatures lay. The judge then asked each of the girls the only question he deemed important: "Girls, do you promise to love your mommies forever and ever?"

They each replied yes with a bright-eyed smile and a twinkle in their eyes. It was over. We were now seen as valid parents in the eyes of the law.

On that day, we didn't become more of a family—we already had that. We did, however, gain the privileges that our straight friends take for granted. I could now sign legal documents for all three of my daughters. We could now sign the line that says "parent." We could take any or all of the girls to school, the pediatrician, or the hospital and make decisions on behalf of them as their legal parents. It's not the signature line that matters—it's being seen, respected, and acknowledged for who I am and who we are as a family.

Cindy and I each hold a kind of "dual legal status" in relation to our girls, where the terms "biological" and "adoptive" mother are both relevant titles to each of us. This has provided a few challenging moments, and a few funny ones.

One of the funny moments happened the day our eldest daughter, Ali, was at the Department of Motor Vehicles to get her drivers' license. Upon arrival, Cindy and Ali were suddenly separated as Ali was guided to another area of the office. Moments before they were separated, Cindy handed Ali the folder with the needed legal documentation. Walking down the corridor, Ali opened the file—and to her surprise, staring right at her was an official "Adoption Certificate" from the state of New York. A look of profound shock came over her and she mouthed to Cindy through the glass window, "I'm adopted?!?"

It was a funny exchange. Of course, she knew that Cindy was her biological mother and that we were both her parents. She also knew about the legal procedure in New York when she was seven years old. The word "adopted" was a new status and identity for her. She had not ever connected that word to her identity. That day in December

2004 had no specific significance to Ali, as it changed nothing. It was a significant day for us as her parents, as the law then "caught up" to our family status. Ali was part of a new club, and at the age of sixteen, she was beginning to understand how the laws had treated her family as "less than."

The Club

I was born into a club
I worked my way into a few others
I am readily invited into some and excluded from more

I am bothered by a few
Impassioned by others

Saddened to learn that some come with rights and privileges
Others are marked by the absence

Rights and privileges for others
But my membership is limited

The subtle and strong messages that say keep out!

Many have sought to keep us out of the parents club and the marriage club. Excluding us from these privileges has always felt punitive and misguided.

One of the things that I was keenly aware of as a young child was that I wanted to, in my adult life, live somewhere other than where I grew up. I craved a level of diversity that I didn't see or experience in my hometown. That's not a critique of the people that I grew up with or where I was raised. In fact, I'm really proud of my hometown. I love the people, and I'm still connected to friends from my childhood and my high school years. I have only good feelings from and about those years and the community of Lakewood, Ohio. It is the place where I learned to work hard, laugh, play, and love my friends and family. However, back then, it wasn't very diverse, and I craved the learning and expansion that comes from a diverse environment.

I attended St. Rose, a Catholic elementary and junior high school. It was here that I expanded my love of learning, connection to God, and value for deep friendship. My head, heart, and soul were nurtured in those eight years by great teachers and friends. In the fall of eighth grade, a priest approached me on the playground—that's a big deal, especially when it's the pastor of the church!

He said, "Hey, I understand you're planning to go to a public high school."

I respectfully replied, "Yes, Father."

He continued, "Well, what would you think if we paid for you to go to the Catholic high school? You are one of our best and brightest students, and we would like you to continue your education at a Catholic school."

At the age of fourteen, I looked directly into his eyes and said, "No, thank you. I really want to attend a public high school."

My response to him surprised both of us: I'd said no to four years of a private high school education. I had been in a very homogeneous environment for eight years of my education, and I craved different. Other than a few of my neighborhood friends, all of my friends were white, Catholic, and from similar economic backgrounds. At fourteen, I instinctually needed different. Today, I have the knowledge and life experience to know why.

I went on to attend a large, public high school, Lakewood High School. It is the place where I discovered my love for writing, running, and academic rigor. I made dear friends, lifetime friends, who know me and love me for who I am. They never judge me for who I am not. My choice to attend Lakewood High School was great for me.

One thing that has remained true for me throughout my life is a deep relationship with God, the term I use to describe our maker. I am saddened and disappointed that people have used and continue to use religion as a way to minimize people who are lesbian, gay, bisexual, or transgender. I don't like that people judge those who practice their faith through a different religious or spiritual practice.

I remember a moment, an interaction I had with my sister, shortly after we had moved to the East Coast. I was talking to her about a church that we'd joined; it happened to be a Methodist church.

She paused, looked me directly in the eyes, and said, "Shelly, aren't you Catholic anymore?"

I realized that, for me, God is not any specific religion. God is everywhere, and most importantly, God is love. That was a really important insight for me.

I replied by saying that of course there is a part of my identity that is Catholic, as this is where I learned so many foundational values and principles that guide my life. And, I have come to believe that God is more universal than that. God is not owned by a specific religion.

When we selected the community in which we would raise our

girls, we wanted it to be represented by a range of faiths, cultures, races, and economic statuses. We chose our school district for its diversity as well as its academic excellence. Our girls have friends from various cultural, religious, and sexual orientations.

We have dear friends and family friends in our community who represent a range of religious faiths. They all, however, believe in respect and love and our shared humanity above any dogma. We have been embraced, supported, and loved by these friends. Unconditionally. We respect their life and spiritual choices and beliefs, and they respect ours.

We have also been judged and dismissed by some. I feel it. I sense it. I have been told. I have experienced it, and so have our children. I have felt disappointed and sad. I have reflected on it, but never been destroyed by it. The fact that some have used God as the basis for their judgment and rejection is very difficult for me to understand. They reference God as the reason why they don't see us as a "valid family" deserving of the same rights and privileges as their family. I don't understand or accept this logic. The God that I know is loving, all loving and all inclusive, and created the differences among us as a way to learn.

All of us in the LGBTQ+ community have encountered people like this. They miss the goodness and grace that resides in human beings who are a part of this community. They miss the unique gifts of so many. They think they have the gateway to God, and that by dismissing us, they can exercise that gateway pass more easily, more seamlessly, and without sin. Or maybe it just feels good for some to judge others. It makes them feel good about themselves. I don't know. I invite them to consider that all pathways lead to God, as he loves without condition. And maybe it's possible that we all have the gateway to God.

The Gateway to God

They think they have
The gateway to God

As if my path
Is any less real
Than their path

My God
The one in my heart
Values the expansion of love
For all

Their God
Judges—critiques
And creates divides
Between his people

When will they see
We are all God's children
Granted the same
Gateway to God
Unconditionally

Those few distinctions have helped me tremendously. For me, God isn't Catholic or any other specific religion. God is love, and no one has the exclusive gateway to God. We all have it. That's been my journey. I have not and I will not tell another how to believe nor what to believe in any arena, particularly one as personal as faith. I do, however, ask anyone who believes that we are "less than," to reconsider the belief that drove that conclusion. Equality and respect never have "less than" at the core.

———————

What is the basis of your relationship with God? With others?

———

What judgments did you inherit?

———

Is there room to expand your views?

———

Are there ingrained belief systems getting in the way of you being authentic and encouraging others to do the same?

9. Connected by Love

Be patient and show them that love has no boundaries.

My deepest insight, after all these years of writing, speaking, and engaging with people from around the world, is that we are all connected by love. There are many experiences that have etched this truth into my heart and soul. But there are two that stand out above the rest.

In July 2014, after thirty years and three daughters, I married my best friend and life partner. Cindy and I were married in Provincetown, Massachusetts, on the deck of The Red Inn. It was just the five of us. It felt right to be just us.

For most couples, this day represents a beginning, but for us, it was about closure. I finally felt free. Free to be me. Free to be us. I felt validated, acknowledged, and loved—without condition. I felt included in a club that had fought so hard to keep me—to keep us—out. It was a new day for me, and for us as a couple, and for our girls.

We exchanged vows and I looked over at our girls. Ali had tears streaming down her face. Kate was smiling ear to ear. And then there was Nicole—she stood there, "clapping and clapping."

"Why isn't anyone else clapping?" she asked.

(She had no recollection of the wish she had made way back when she was four years old, which made this moment so stunning!)

After a private and fun lunch (thanks to the champagne and dessert sent by dear friends), we headed for the door. I looked back to find Cindy in deep conversation with a hotel employee.

Jorge had approached Cindy with tears in his eyes: "That was the most beautiful thing I've ever witnessed. So much joy. So much love. I hope that I, too, can have that someday. True love. Children. A family to call my own. As a gay man, it's not easy for me to believe I can have all of that. You gave me hope and inspiration."

We were so happy that we could give Jorge something that eluded us for so many years. There had been so many messages telling us that our love was less valid, less real. That was now all behind us.

After a celebration at the beach, we drove about two hours to be with Cindy's family. It was so important to all of us that we celebrate with my now "official" mother-in-law, Alice. She had always been relentless and persistent in her support and love for us.

That night, as the five of us said goodnight to her, she looked up at me and quietly whispered, "Shelly—I am SO HAPPY."

I looked back at her, smiled, and said, "I know you are—so am I."

I'm glad we could give her this joy before she left this Earth.

Alice passed away two years later in 2016 at the age of ninety-seven. The five of us sat with her in her final days and moments on Earth. It gave us the chance to give back the love she so generously gave us for so many years. A woman of great strength and deep love. The best mother-in-law anyone could ever have.

Everyone deserves to have hope and happiness. To believe that they can have the life they want—to have the love they feel acknowledged and seen as valid and valuable. It is time to open hearts and minds, to create space for everyone to live the lives they were meant to live. I believe that who we are—our unique natures, strengths, insights, and gifts—is so much more powerful and relevant than any label someone can throw at us or on us. Labels limit. Love expands.

Labels

We limit with our labels

We assume who people are
And what they like to do

We overvalue the what
We undervalue the who

We miss the gifts
Given to each

We miss the purpose and path
Each came to pursue

What will it take
To meet, connect, and discover

Who you are
Who we are

Who we can be together
. . . I Believe We Can Be Very Powerful Together!

My mother-in-law knew that Cindy and I had spent decades without the privilege of a title or a label that included or embraced us. Eleven years earlier, in 2005, we experienced a beautiful moment of validation. She offered that validation in her sweet, thoughtful, but very direct manner. Alice, then eighty-six years old, became the first person ever to introduce me properly.

"This is my daughter-in-law, Shelly," she said to a neighbor.

It was particularly meaningful because, back in 2005, after twenty years together, we couldn't legally marry. We were, however, connected by love, commitment, and three, beautiful daughters. Alice, my mother-in-law, didn't need a law to properly define our relationship. She acknowledged us for who we were to her and to each other. No blanks. No pauses.

No Blanks, No Pauses

We don't usually get the privilege
Of a title or label that includes and embraces us

We get the pause and the blanks
"This is Shelly and . . . uhhh, Cindy."
It's the kind of pause that forces the listener to wonder
Who I am and how I fit in

The realization usually settles in as they see me with my
partner and kids
That all changed one rainy day in May

Sweet, loving, 86 year old Alice introduced me to a neighbor:
"This is my daughter-in-law, Shelly."
No blanks, no pauses

Only love and genuine acknowledgement
Of who I was to her

No blanks, no pauses

To Alice, I was her daughter-in-law. The laws and courts would catch up to her later.

It's moments like these that give me hope. She had a choice to make, and she was very clear about her decision. She chose to acknowledge me. She chose to love us. No Blanks. No Pauses.

My sister, Mary Lou, was also the embodiment of love. She loved without conditions, without restrictions, and without the expectation of getting anything in return. She showed love to everyone, always.

I had my final conversation with my sister on March 22, 2017. Mary Lou passed away on April 2. Words can't express the depth of pain I felt upon her passing.

The last words I spoke to my sister? "I love you forever."

She smiled back at me.

The last words she spoke to me? "I picked out the poem, Shelly. It's in the book. I highlighted it."

The clarity of her statement left me speechless. She was so clear and focused for someone in her final days with brain cancer. I was stunned by her ability to speak and by what she said. My sister knew that I was a writer and that I wrote poems, among other things.

I went home and opened my book of poems. I instantly knew which poem she had selected as her favorite.

I read this poem as part of her service. She'd chosen it; I had to share it. I wanted to honor her, as she so selflessly honored all who knew her by loving without condition or restriction. I realized that I'd taken her love for granted. She gave her love so freely, so generously. I so hope that she felt the deep love I had for her.

When my sister passed away, I was preparing to begin posting my writing online. The piece that she'd selected was one that I had written many years earlier. It wasn't until then that I realized it was she who taught me that "we are all connected by love." She chose love. I wonder how different our world would be if we all chose love? I dedicate this to my dear sister, Mary Lou.

We Are All Connected

Death taught me how to Live
With Purpose

Sickness gave me Appreciation of
True Health

Loss reminded me how to Live
And Laugh

You showed me that we are
All Connected

By Love

I believe the struggle is *our* struggle, not yours or mine. Victory is when we all feel free to live and be our whole selves.

Differences require us to accept people for who they are—not who we want them to be. I encourage you to make choices from a place of love and support others in pursuing the same. When we choose to judge less and love more, anything is possible.

⚶——⚶⚬⚶——⚶

I encourage you to:
Level Set; see each of us as different, but equally magnificent.

⚶⚬⚶

Live Authentically; live true to who you are. No hiding. No apology.

⚶⚬⚶

No Blanks. No Pauses. For anyone.

⚶⚬⚶

Make Choices that are consistent with who you are and what you want out of life. Make choices from a place of love.

10. Reflections

Life Stages now past. The quiet and stillness left behind . . .

I am in a new phase of my life. I know that my path and purpose have brought me to this place and this moment. I am grateful for the journey, the people, and the lessons that have shaped me along the way.

As I write the final pages of this book, I am a few days away from being appointed Chief Diversity & Inclusion Officer at Procter & Gamble—a great honor, an even greater responsibility. I have been called to help shape the culture, policies, and leadership in a company that serves more than 4.6 billion consumers and more than 90,000 employees around the world.

There is something very comforting about landing in a spot that feels like the exact place you were meant to be. I work for a company that is committed to making all employees feel valued and included. We see inclusion as a business choice and business imperative. We are not perfect—but in our imperfection, we are committed to respecting all.

I have more people in my life that I love than I have time to see.

Cindy and I have built a home of love together. We are also in the midst of a family transition. Our youngest, our twins, left for college a few months ago; our eldest daughter is in her third year of college. We have officially become empty nesters. I am not yet used to being in this club. I have come to appreciate the quiet, but I am saddened by the silence.

I Hear the Silence

I hear the silence
In the hallway

I didn't know
That silence
Had sound

But it does

The pitter-patter
Of toddlers
The laughter
Of children
The sassiness
Of teenagers

No more

Life stages
Now past
The quiet and stillness
Left behind for us to hear

I am saddened
By the silence

The silence came fast. Our home, our life was created with such intentionality, and from a place of deep love. The place and space that has kept me feeling safe and whole is shifting in ways that leave me feeling a bit empty and sad. The physical absence of our girls leaves a deep void.

I miss our girls. I miss their voices, their laughter, and their hugs. Nothing prepared me for this silence or this feeling of loss. The home base of their lives feels like it is now elsewhere. Their lives and lists of commitments are taking them in many different directions. Our lives are diverging.

On one of those quiet Sunday afternoons in the spring of 2019, I went in search of some memories to reground me. I opened the big box where I keep special cards and letters. It's not ordered or organized in any way; I was fortunate and relieved to find words they had each written either about or directly to us.

I found the letters that Kate and Nicole had each written to us at the end of their senior year in high school. It is a tradition and ritual led by thoughtful teachers and school administrators, prompting our girls to capture their feelings and appreciation at an important life transition. I wanted and needed to hear from Ali, so I went in search of the essay she wrote for her college application. I found her essay, and after sharing it with Ali after those many years, she shared this piece she wrote with me. On this cloudy, rainy Sunday afternoon, I absorbed every last word I read from my three daughters.

Excerpts from our girls' letters and essays:

Dear Cin & Shell,

Wow. I don't even know where to begin. I cannot thank you enough for all that you have done for me over the last 18 years. I would not be who I am today without your endless love and support.

You have never failed to make me feel encouraged and always help me understand what's important. I truly feel like all you've wanted for me is success and happiness.

In addition to all of the little kind things you've done, like dropping off a homework assignment or packing my lunch, you've also made sure I always felt so loved.

School and life can be busy and difficult, and you have helped me build confidence in all areas of my life and my abilities. I also appreciate the trust you have put in me to make my own decisions and how you've let/helped me mature over the years.

All I know is that I am going to truly miss you both so much next year. I will be so sad to not come home to this loving house that I call my home. Though we have all had difficult moments, I wouldn't change anything about it.

As I graduate, I want to make sure you knew how special you are to me. I could not have made it without you.

Love Always . . . Kate

Cintin and Shellbell,

When I thought about writing this letter, my initial feeling was that this seemed a little silly. A small card won't allow me to thank you for the past 18 years of my life. It is something I will never be able to repay.

Even when it seemed like I didn't care, your actions, from warming my car in the morning to attending my track meets, never went unnoticed or unappreciated.

You taught me things I will take with me for the rest of my life. You have given me endless opportunities, pushed me to be better, and shown me unwavering support.

I can't wait to make you proud. This is a time full of so many emotions, and it's the time when you begin to see that little girl from the home videos has started to grow up.

I love you more than words can express and I only hope you're proud of who I am becoming.

Xoxox...... Nicole

As a young, insecure, shy girl, having two moms was something I felt quite embarrassed about. It was something I often tried to hide. I didn't want the other kids to know. I didn't want them to see me differently. I heard comments and phrases at recess. Kids say mean things. I know now that we were all trying to discover who we were, and it wasn't their fault that they were repeating derogatory comments used by an entire generation before us. It still hurt.

Those moments of embarrassment turned into moments of guilt. I felt guilty for having these feelings and for wanting to hide my parents. My parents had showed me nothing but love and support, so why did I want to hide them? It was a battle between my head and my heart that went on for years. Until one day, things changed. I realized how much of a gift this was. It was a unique perspective that suddenly made me feel special. Instead of hiding my parents, I now feel excited to tell people and share my parents and family.

For many, I am the first person they have met with lesbian moms. People have questions, and I can see in their eyes if there is a veil of judgement or pure curiosity. (I've found more of the latter.) I enjoy opening up to people and teaching them that I'm not so different than them, that my childhood was, at the root of it, not so different from theirs.

The only difference was that I was taught from the moment I was born the direct impact and importance of acceptance, advocacy, and unconditional love for all.

It wasn't always easy; it wasn't always what I wanted. But as I grew older, I realized that all the things that made it hard were the same things that made me a better person.

Having two moms has been the best gift of my life. They have taught me unconditional love. They have taught me acceptance. They have taught me to look past initial barriers and labels that make us seem so different. That underneath, we are all human, and we are more alike than different.

My moms are my greatest gift, and I couldn't be prouder.

...... Ali

I sat with the letters in my lap, tears streaming down my face. I felt peace. I felt pride. We did our job as parents. We sent three strong, independent young women into the world. Their presence will make a difference. Their lives will make a difference. I am grateful to be a mom and to have these three girls as our daughters. I am proud of the journey we travelled together that has sown love deeply into all of our hearts. Those three little girls from the home videos are all grown up.

I am also learning that grief and gratitude can co-exist. They serve to balance each other—or maybe it is the existence of one that validates the other. My deep grief lets me know that what Cindy and I created together is good—it matters. I am grieving the time and special moments we had as a family. And yet, while the silence saddens me, the strength, wisdom, and independence of these young women invigorates me.

I recall the judge from Family Court in New York on Adoption Day and the question he asked of Ali, Kate, and Nicole: "Hey girls, I have only one question for you—do you promise to love your mommies forever and ever?"

"Yes!" they replied in unison.

He knew then what we have learned over the many years since—it is the love between us that matters most.

Writing this book and sharing my stories and poetry has helped me heal. The process of writing and sharing has further expanded my heart and mind. It's been good to go back in time and relive experiences and feelings from long ago. I have processed feelings and thoughts that have held me hostage to fear, insecurity, anger, and judgment. I feel more free and peaceful. I didn't expect that.

I am grateful for all of the teachers along my journey—those who brought me pain as well as those who healed my wounds and calmed my fears. A special thank you to those who believed in me when I didn't. Encouraged me when I gave up. Supported me when I wasn't in the room. And said the words I needed to hear when few cared or had enough courage to speak them to me. You changed me for the better.

Thank you to Cindy, my soulmate. She has loved me for more than thirty-five years. Life takes many twists and turns. She never gave up on me and always loved me. Ali, Kate, and Nicole—you are more than enough for us. I love these four humans with every ounce of my being. Always.

I hope that you, the reader, discovered something in these pages that supports you on your journey. I hope you are inspired to bring more love into the world. I believe that my life's purpose is to open hearts, open minds, and build connections that heal the world. My sense is that the world could use more love and healing right now. Don't you?

Acknowledgments

I have deep gratitude for all who guided, supported, and encouraged me in the creation of this book. I have many to thank.

First, to my wife Cindy, for knowing exactly the words I needed to include or delete to ensure the book and words stayed anchored in respect, integrity, and love. All are personal traits she embodies.

To Kate, our daughter and my first editor, who offered the framing and sequence that gave the book the grounding and flow it so needed.

To Ali, our daughter, for her instinct to know that my childhood home belonged on the cover. Ali's creative guidance led me to a cover that grounded me and the words.

To Nicole, our daughter, for reminding me every time I hit a roadblock (and there were many), "You got this, Mo (Mom)." She believed in me.

To my mother, who believed in me and loved me without condition, always. It was Mom who laid the foundation of love I so heavily rely on every day of my life.

To my brothers and sisters, for giving me a base of love and family: Brian, Kathleen, Maureen, Dan, Mary Lou, Margaret Ann, Francis, Patrick, Tim, Loretta, Jean, Nancy, Tom, and Mary Ellen. And to their spouses, who loved and supported me throughout the years.

To my nieces and nephews (too many to name here), for giving me a base of love and family, and the great honor of being an aunt to all of them.

To my in-laws, for their endless love and support of me, Cindy, and the family we created together: Deb, Steve, John, Rick, Rob, Dave, Josh, Derrick, Scott, Ben, Keith, and Diana.

To my guide, coach, adviser, and dear friend, Kelly Vanasse. Kelly, the sherpa with genius, grit, and heart. Kelly gave me advice at literally every step of my journey. She gave selflessly and consistently. She answered every phone call, text, and email. We started this journey together, meeting on Sunday mornings for breakfast at The Sleepy Bee Café. It was here that Kelly gave me the roadmap and inspiration I needed to write and to publish this book.

To Jaime Schaeffer, my dear friend, guide, coach, social media adviser, and so many other things. Jaime was tenacious at keeping me focused on "the next step." Jaime offered practical steps and unique insight that got me over every hurdle. Jaime sacrificed weekend time with her kids to work on this project with me. She made the difficult things seem easy.

To my dear friend and colleague, Marc Pritchard. Marc stood by me and with me. He believed in me and my desire to expand my voice and reach. He connected me to people and ideas that offered me the "missing piece" I so needed but didn't know. Marc taught me that respect, equality, and goodness are essential ingredients for the growth of communities, companies, and economies. He is a role model, willing to both follow and to lead—always with compassion and humility.

To John Pepper, for his wisdom and input on my early manuscript. His guidance and questions shifted my thinking in important ways. I saved every email of encouragement he sent me. There are many.

To those who have been by my side in this work and in my life—

Deanna Bass, Kevin Bleyle, Nancy Brown-Jamison, Maria Decordova, Crystal Harrell, Cheryl Gray Hines, Maureen Howard, Clare Iery, Vinitaa Jayson, Debbie Kruse, Patrice Louvet, Debbie Majoras, David Martin, Meg McCann, Barb Miller, Brent Miller, Mary Pickering, Ed Shirley, Tamara Thomas, Brenda Villa, and Charlene Zappa.

To David Taylor and Jon Moeller, for building a company, culture, and business strategy that supports and values the full breadth of humanity.

To my P&G colleagues who are members of our LGBTQ+ community and our allies: This group of people created an environment where all of us can bring our full selves to work. They built a community for learning and a community for sharing. They nurtured and developed great talent. They created a model for allyship and respect. They did the courageous and challenging work required to shift our systems, policies, and culture to be more inclusive for our community and all employees. And, they encouraged me to step up and speak out. They created a platform where I shared my words, stories, and passion for progress.

To the many P&G leaders around the world for creating a vision, culture, and space for equality to be at the center of our conversation. For your commitment to make P&G one of the most innovative, diverse, and inclusive companies in the world. P&G provided a container for me to grow, learn, experiment, speak, write, and give voice to respect and inclusion within a corporation, as well as outside its walls. To those of you who have built systems and cultures that continue to put access and opportunity for all as a central tenet and for those of you who have stood by my side as friend, confidant, co-worker, manager, and advocate: You individually and collectively contributed to the inspiration, encouragement, and support I needed to bring this book to life. In July 2020, my title changed to Chief Equality & Inclusion Officer, reflecting an evolution in our company strategy—our clear commitment to the outcomes of equality and inclusion for all.

To the educational institutions that offered me knowledge, insight, teachers who cared, and communities of learning, it is these experiences and people that accelerated my growth as a human being and as a professional: St. Rose School, Lakewood High School, The University of Michigan, and Case Western Reserve University. Within their walls I transformed into a student of life and humanity.

To my Lakewood High School crew, for your lifetime of friendship and love—Sheila Dugan, Kit Hoffert, Kathy Nortz Lanese, Kim Lewis, Laurie Casey Moline, and Jennifer Woomer.

To our special Sycamore friends and neighbors, for your endless support and encouragement—Patsy DiGiovanna, Renee Gottliebson, Kathy Jensen, Holly Kuhnell, Bari Thornberry, Melissa Weiss, Lyn and John Manos, Karen and Jeff Greenberger, and Stacey and Jay Bolotin.

To Krista Jones Gehring and Iain Jones, for being my first photographers and website designers. You offered your creative gifts graciously and selflessly.

To Eric Scheer, for his wisdom and creative work on my website. You believed in the mission. You trusted my intentions and plans.

To Patrick McGilvray, the website guru who made every technical and design change look easy.

To Michael Iery, for his filming and video expertise, passion and commitment to equality.

To my editor, Lauren Kanne, for her wisdom, patience, and laughter. Lauren instinctively knew what the manuscript, or the author, needed to keep moving. Lauren has a rare combination of brilliance, patience, and humor. I admire her gifts.

To Naren Aryal, Matt Gonsalves, Jess Cohn, Nicole Hall, Anna-

Marie Mapes, Kristin Perry, Bridget Blakely, and the rest of the team at Amplify Publishing, for their endless patience as I iterated and evolved. They offered me the space and support I needed at each stage in the creation process.

And finally, to my mother in-law, Alice, for inspiring the title of this book. In her time on this Earth, she gave meaning and significance to the words "No Blanks, No Pauses."

Original Poems
by Shelly McNamara

In this section you will find the poems that are scattered throughout my book. They are perforated to better enable your reflection and enjoyment.

Deep Insight

Deep insight is rarely
Born out of privilege
It comes from
Experiencing the pain
Caused by others—or
The misgivings of life

Listen closely
Listen intently
To the voices
Of those who cry out

They sit along the edges
Outside the circle
Of privilege

Deep insight they bring
How we can all
Be more human
More loving—more giving

Deep insight is rarely
Born out of privilege

Shelly McNamara

Or So They Say

The wind was blowing—the leaves falling
Another hour, another day
Another life—and who's to blame?
The night was ceasing—God was calling
He watches us all—or so they say

The factor was timing—the driver was drinking
A door opened, a door closed
The life was hers—and why not his?
The sirens were ringing—people were crying
He always keeps order—or so they say

My life was growing—hers was going
If only then, if only now
Why not me—and why not you?
The questions were coming—answers were lacking
He has his reasons—or so they say

Still we are living—but not understanding
No longer questioning—but rather accepting
It was her time—her own special time

We have all grown—we have all changed
By having known her, loved her, and lost her

Shelly McNamara

Until Then

We will always remember . . .
Your face—handsome and angelic
Your smile—innocent, yet deeply knowing
Your kindness—you gave just by being
Your tin whistle & fiddle—you lightened our spirits
Your contagious Irish laugh
Your heart—you loved us and we loved you
Your gentle loving spirit

You are a child of God
Now in the arms of the Lord
Rest in His peace
Rest in His love

It's only a moment until we are together again . . .
Until then, we will remember . . .
I love you, Kevin.
Aunt Shelly

Shelly McNamara

I Learned

Maybe it's in the loss
That I've learned to give

From rejection
I learned to embrace

In the judgment
I learned to accept

In the dishonor
I learned to love and honor all

In the end
I learned to love you and me

Shelly McNamara

The Mystery Man

Now, seeing the mystery man
Hardly mentioned, spoken, or heard of
The mythical man not to be seen

Today, here and now, looking into your saddened eyes
Pain wells up inside me—I dare to breathe

To recreate a past of twenty years
To tell you of the thousand times I asked myself—why?

Now, I see the pain and the tears
Held so tightly within this God-sent woman—my mother

How to view, name, or call one a father?

Shelly McNamara

Is it Time to Forgive?

How do you say goodbye
To someone you never knew
Never saw
Never loved

How do you forgive someone
Who never apologized
For the pain
The suffering
The absence

How do you learn
To trust again

Once they walk out on you
The pain stays
Trust impossible to find

Dear father, you left a void
A chasm no one could ever fill

Do you need me to forgive and say goodbye?
Or do I?

Shelly McNamara

Dear Brother – Dear Sister

Thank you for stepping in
For giving love
And safety

No one could know
The pain
The void
The loss

Felt only when
A parent walks
Out on you

The pain is too much
The void is too deep

There is never goodbye for us

I love you
Forever

Shelly McNamara

Blinded

What will it take for you to
See me as I am

To see the gifts I have been given
Just as you and yours

We miss each other
We walk past
We overlook

We never see
What each of us really has or is

Blinded by our notion of
What or who we should be

Shelly McNamara

Brian Joseph McNamara

A restless soul
Always seemed to have somewhere to go or something to do
A restless soul now quieted, safe, and at home with his maker

Our hearts are heavy
Our hearts are sad

But lightened by knowing that when our Mother passes on—soon
She will be met at the Gates of Heaven by her first-born son
Brian, always with a special place in Mom's heart
Now there to greet her and bring her home

Brian Joseph McNamara, dear brother
Forget what we didn't say or didn't do in this lifetime together
There's always a special place in our heart for you

Rest in peace, dear brother. We love you very much.

Shelly McNamara

I Regret

If I were to wish
For anything

If I were to
Regret anything

I wish that I had
Loved more and
Judged less

I just didn't see it
Didn't see you

I regret

Shelly McNamara

You Have Been Chosen

The day will come
The moment will pass
When you will be called as different
In a way that says "Less"
Less than

We will be waiting
To step in
To give you the love
To remind you of the reason

That God made you special
Gave you two moms

He called you to teach
Love One Another
Not One
But All

You are the chosen teachers
We are the committed parents
Always there
To remind you

Why you have been chosen to lead

Shelly McNamara

Next Time

Next time—you might regret
The times you walked past me
The times you looked away

Next time—I might not be here
To hear your sorrows
To forgive your regrets
To heal your wounds

Next time—you might really miss me
Because I may be gone

We might not have a next time

Shelly McNamara

Love Makes A Family

What If I told you that
Love makes a family
That God places children
With parents he chooses

That your view of love
Doesn't match mine

That I have a love for my children
That drowns out your judgment
Your exclusion of me as a parent worthy to serve

I answered my call
What about you?

Shelly McNamara

They Crossed the Line

They crossed the line
One by one
"If you have ever been made fun of for being . . .
Black—Overweight—Jewish—or Gay

Cross the line

If you have ever been called a 'sissy' or soft for
Crying—showing your feelings
Or showing you care

Cross the line

Cross the line of pain

The line we all created
The place we taught our children to go
And send others

To dump their feelings of fear and self-doubt

We created the world and line of bigotry
How can we erase it?

Shelly McNamara

The Day I Lost A Friend

The day I lost a friend ...
I was smiling, bright and happy
I was caring and concerned for others
I was myself

And then I lost my friend
She liked me for my laughter, insights and caring ways
But her smile soon faded
And so too did her friendship

All that I had said
All that I had done
All that I was to her
Lost ... in a moment's time

All because of who I am
And because of that, I lost my friend

Shelly McNamara

Can You Let Me in Now?

Time passes
Life passes
Why focus on things that bring distance between us?

I pass by you daily
Do I see, acknowledge, and celebrate you?

Do I judge what you are, who you see, and how you look?

Our lives have kept us apart
My judgment has kept us apart

I am older and wiser now
I see you so rarely
I wish to see you more

I long to share a moment with you
If only to share a smile or word of advice
Or maybe a tear for all of the time and
Pain that has passed

I once passed you by with only a frown and a scorn
As I judged what you were
Who you saw and
How you looked

If only I had known what is so clear to me now
All of those years since past

Can you let me in now?

Shelly McNamara

Level Set

We are taught to see things and people
As better than and less than

Why not "different than?"

We have this need to level up and down
I win—you lose
You win—I lose
One up—one down
Always

Why not "level set?"
Grant you space to be you
And I get to be me

We no longer need
To make one better than
To make one "less than"

What will it take to "level set?"
To see each other as different
But equally magnificent

Create space where everyone can shine

Shelly McNamara

The Gift of Freedom

Among so many other things, little peanut
You've given me freedom
Given us freedom

It's an inner strength, an inner peace
I've never before felt
I've never before known

It's an outer voice to claim what's mine
To take what's mine
To take what's ours

It's the space to make our family
The voice to name our love
The calm to live amidst the storm
That inevitably awaits us
As those around us miss the message of God
Miss the message of love

We live our lives more fully—more connected
We share our love more openly—more freely
It's you that grant us this gift
The gift to know, love, and publicly be oneself
The true gift of freedom

Shelly McNamara

A Letter for My Daughters

There will be those who will not like you
They will scorn, frown, and resent
Your very existence

They will pass you by, mock, tease, and never invite you
To their birthday parties

They think that gay parents are less than—
With nothing of value to teach

Their eyes are blinded by prejudice, fear, and hatred
Things you never learned from us

We've taught you kindness—share it abundantly
We've given you love, lots of love
Draw from it to keep you whole

We've given you faith, trust, and confidence in God, Self, and Others
You will need them often
Remember, your two moms came together
To create a family and legacy of love
You are an integral part of that plan

Yes, there are those who don't see us in this light
Be patient and show them that love has no boundaries

Shelly McNamara

Peering in From Without

I look from within at the world
In which I find myself
In which we find ourselves

I see faces that choose only to recognize parts of me privately
Parts of me publicly
"This is my son, Jack, his wife, Jill and their darling son, Michael
Uhhh, yeah, and this is my sister, Shelly . . .
And this is Cindy."

The validation—the invalidation
The love they choose to ignore
The pain they never see
Relationships validated
Relationships invalidated

The love they publicly ignore
I privately keep for my own
To nurture, to keep me safe
From a world that forces me to
Peer in from without

Shelly McNamara

Making Choices

When I make choices that are consistent with
Who I am
What I bring
Why I'm here

I live more fully
I live more freely

I am able to accept your choices
Who you are
What you bring
Why you're here

Being more fully me
Allows you to be more fully you
We not only co-exist
We co-create

Shelly McNamara

On the Edges

They think there's one straight line
That takes you down the middle
Of the road

What about the beauty, the excitement
That lies along the edges?

The center line—the straight line
Takes you to the places
You have already been

I invite you to explore the edges
To go outside the lines
To find the beauty
Not on the straight line
To find the beauty that comes
From exploring and living on the edges

This is where I have found the insight
On the edges
Not down the middle of the road

Shelly McNamara

The Club

I was born into a club
I worked my way into a few others
I am readily invited into some and excluded from more

I am bothered by a few
Impassioned by others

Saddened to learn that some come with rights and privileges
Others are marked by the absence

Rights and privileges for others
But my membership is limited

The subtle and strong messages that say keep out!

Shelly McNamara

The Gateway to God

They think they have
The gateway to God

As if my path
Is any less real
Than their path

My God
The one in my heart
Values the expansion of love
For all

Their God
Judges—critiques
And creates divides
Between his people

When will they see
We are all God's children
Granted the same
Gateway to God
Unconditionally

Shelly McNamara

Labels

We limit with our labels

We assume who people are
And what they like to do

We overvalue the what
We undervalue the who

We miss the gifts
Given to each

We miss the purpose and path
Each came to pursue

What will it take
To meet, connect, and discover

Who you are
Who we are

Who we can be together
. . . I Believe We Can Be Very Powerful Together!

Shelly McNamara

No Blanks, No Pauses

We don't usually get the privilege
Of a title or label that includes and embraces us

We get the pause and the blanks
"This is Shelly and . . . uhhh, Cindy."
It's the kind of pause that forces the listener to wonder
Who I am and how I fit in

The realization usually settles in as they see me with my partner and kids
That all changed one rainy day in May

Sweet, loving, 86 year old Alice introduced me to a neighbor:
"This is my daughter-in-law, Shelly."
No blanks, no pauses

Only love and genuine acknowledgement
Of who I was to her

No blanks, no pauses

Shelly McNamara

We Are All Connected

Death taught me how to Live
With Purpose

Sickness gave me Appreciation of
True Health

Loss reminded me how to Live
And Laugh

You showed me that we are
All Connected

By Love

Shelly McNamara

I Hear the Silence

I hear the silence
In the hallway

I didn't know
That silence
Had sound

But it does

The pitter-patter
Of toddlers
The laughter
Of children
The sassiness
Of teenagers

No more

Life stages
Now past
The quiet and stillness
Left behind for us to hear

I am saddened
By the silence

Shelly McNamara